Planning Instruction for Adult Learners

Third Edition

Planning Instruction

For Adult Learners

Third Edition

Patricia Cranton

WE

Wall & Emerson, Inc.
Toronto

All orders to purchase copies of this work should be sent to:

The University of Toronto Press, 5201 Dufferin Street, Toronto, Ontario, Canada M3H 5T8.

Phone: 1-800-565-9523. Fax 1-800-221-9985.

E-mail: utpbooks@utpress.utoronto.ca.

Through Pubnet: SAN 115 1134

Requests for permission to make copies of any part of this work should be sent to:

Wall & Emerson, Inc., 21 Dale Avenue, Suite 533, Toronto, Ontario, Canada M4W 1K3.

Fax and voice messages: (416) 352-5368.

E-mail: wall@wallbooks.com.

Web site: www.wallbooks.com

Library and Archives Canada Cataloguing in Publication

Cranton, Patricia

     Planning instruction for adult learners / Patricia Cranton. -- 3rd ed

Includes bibliographical references and index.
ISBN 978-1-895131-25-3

     1. Adult education. 2. Teaching. I. Title.

LC5219.C73 2012   374'.13   C2011-907879-1

Contents

Preface

Adult educators often undertake the complex task of planning courses in their areas of expertise with very little or no formal preparation on how to teach. Following the format of an established textbook, relying on familiar teaching methods encountered as students, and using the assignments and tests from the back of the book provide some guidance. However, such solutions can be as dissatisfying for the teacher as they inevitably will be for the students. It is my intent in this book to integrate what we know about how adults learn with principles of instructional design to produce a practical, yet theoretically based, guide for planning instruction.

Background

Instructional design has its roots in behaviorism from the 1950s and 1960s and imposes a technical model on a social and political process. Adult education is founded in humanism and critical social theory. In adult education, scholars and practitioners are more likely to talk about program planning than instructional design, but essentially the two processes are parallel. Also, instructional design has since evolved to include constructivist strategies, and it now more comfortably coexists with adult education.

The first edition of this book reflected, in part, a transition in my professional life. At the time when I initially studied education and psychology, behaviorism dominated the scene. We collected baseline counts on students' behavior using bracelets with bead counters. We were excited about the advent of teaching machines and programmed instruction. Educational research rigorously adhered to the scientific method, complete with experimental and control groups. I worked within the paradigm of instructional design for the next 15 years. It was shortly after I moved into the area of adult education that I wrote the first edition of *Planning Instruction for Adult Learners*, founded on both my prior experience and my new interest in adult education.

In the second edition of *Planning Instruction for Adult Learners*, I merged my changed perspectives on adult education (including self-directed learning, transformative learning, and an interest in critical theory) with a more fluid approach to instructional design. I maintained the practical approach to planning instruction, but allowed room for paradoxes, critique, and critical reflection.

In this third edition, I retain all of the characteristics of the book that have led to its popularity in the field in terms of style, content, practicality, and illustrations. However, in the last ten years, the knowledge base in adult education has continued to grow, and I have incorporated those developments into this edition. Adult learning theory has become more holistic; in addition to a focus on the acquisition of cognitive knowledge, adult learning theory now includes embodied learning, narrative learning, and spirituality. North American educators are also now drawing on non-Western perspectives on learning and postmodern ways of knowing. Critical theory has taken a firm place in adult education. I have incorporated these trends in the text.

Two other significant developments have shaped the field of adult education in the last ten years. One is that transformative learning theory and research has expanded dramatically including a comprehensive text on how practitioners can teach for transformation (Mezirow and Taylor, 2009) and a handbook on transformative learning (Taylor and Cranton, 2012). The second significant change has been the proliferation of online teaching and learning, primarily in higher education settings, but also in other adult education settings such as the workplace. There are elements of planning instruction for online use that differ from those for a face-to-face course, and this is incorporated into the third edition.

Purpose and Audience

It is my purpose in this book to present a practical procedure by which educators can plan instruction for adults, regardless of the context within which that instruction takes place. I include all aspects of the planning process, from the initial consideration of the learners through to evaluating the success of the instruction.

The objectives of the book are to:

- introduce some of the many learner characteristics relevant to planning instruction;
- provide clear guidelines for writing objectives for and with learners;
- suggest techniques for sequencing topics in instruction;
- help educators select methods that will promote different kinds of learning;
- give an overview of instructional materials and criteria for when to use them;
- offer strategies for giving good feedback to students;
- present concrete technical advice on how to construct tests and evaluative learning projects; and,
- propose a framework and specific procedures for evaluating instruction.

Anyone who teaches adults will find this book useful. Beginning educators will find a concrete procedure for planning workshops, classes, and courses. Experienced educators will find an overall framework within which they can fit many of the things they already do and new suggestions to hone their expertise in designing instruction.

Planning Instruction for Adult Learners has been used for more than twenty years as a textbook in college and university courses on teaching adults. This third edition will continue to serve that audience.

Overview of the Contents

In Chapter One, *Theoretical Framework*, I define instructional design and adult education, and discuss the integration of the two. I review the theoretical foundation of adult education, beginning with John Dewey and Eduard Lindeman and then lead into recent theoretical work in adult learning and adult development.

In Chapter Two, *Considering the Learners*, I describe characteristics of learners that can be taken into account in the planning of instruction. The more we know about our students, the better we can facilitate their learning. It is helpful to be aware of basic characteristics of our learners, such as their work experience, cultural background, and professional goals. Attention needs to be paid to diversity (race, ethnicity, gender, and sexual orientation) and learning style.

One of the first steps in planning instruction is to select the topics to be included and consider our goals and objectives (preferably through working with learners). In Chapter Three, *Objectives*, I review the basics of creating good objectives, provide an overview of different types of learning, and discuss how to involve adult learners in the development of objectives.

In Chapter Four, *Sequencing Learning*, I present guidelines for planning the order or structure of the learning experiences. Some disciplines, such as mathematics and science, have a clear, natural structure. We know that some topics have to be learned before others can be attempted; concepts depend on or incorporate each other. However, this natural structure is not obvious in many subjects. How do we determine the appropriate sequence of learning? How can students be involved in structuring their own learning?

In Chapter Five, *Selecting Methods*, I review many of the methods available to the adult educator. The selection of appropriate instructional strategies may well be the most complex decision in planning instruction. The choices are dependent on, among many other factors, the characteristics of the learner, the nature of the expected learning, the size of the group, the facilities available, and our own skills and preferences as instructors. Planning for online teaching and the selection of strategies available is a new section in this chapter.

We may not often think about the importance of the instructional materials we use in teaching. We hand out or post an electronic copy of a reading and perhaps use a PowerPoint presentation. But why a reading? Why a PowerPoint? In Chapter Six, *Selecting Materials*, I review the common forms instructional materials can take, analyze their strengths and weaknesses, and provide guidelines for selecting materials based on the requirements of the learning task.

The planning, selection, and development of techniques to evaluate learning, whether for feedback or grading, are addressed in Chapter Seven, *Evaluating Learning*. Deciding how to evaluate learning is based on the nature of the learning, some characteristics of the students, and the setting within which we work.

In Chapter Eight, *Evaluating Instruction*, I describe a procedure for assessing the quality of the instruction. Being aware of the effectiveness of our teaching is as important as, and related to, being cognizant of the quality and depth of our students' learning. Included in this chapter is a section on teaching portfolios, including e-portfolios.

The Author

Patricia Cranton received her B.Ed. degree (1971) and M.Sc. degree (1973) from the University of Calgary, and her Ph.D. degree (1976) from the University of Toronto in measurement, evaluation, and computer applications.

Patricia's main research interests have been in the areas of evaluating teaching in higher education, instructional development, and transformative learning. She was selected as a Distinguished Scholar at Brock University in 1991 in recognition of her research and writing. She received the Ontario Confederation of University Faculty Association's Teaching Award in 1993 and the Lieutenant Governor's Laurel Award in 1994 for an outstanding contribution to university teaching.

Her other books include *Working with Adult Learners* (1992), *Professional Development as Transformative Learning* (1996), *No One Way: Teaching and Learning in Higher Education* (1998), *Personal Empowerment through Type* (1998), *Becoming an Authentic Teacher* (2000) and *Understanding and Promoting Transformative Learning* (2nd Edition) (2006).

Patricia has also edited five *New Directions in Adult and Continuing Education* volumes: *Transformative Learning in Action* (1997), *Universal Challenges in Faculty Work* (1997), *Fresh Approaches to the Evaluation of Teaching* (with Chris Knapper, 2001), *Authenticity in Teaching* (2006), and *Reaching out Across the Boarder: Canadian Perspectives in Adult Education* (with Leona English, 2009).

Patricia Cranton is currently a Professor of Adult Education affiliated with the University of New Brunswick. She has been Professor of Adult Education at Penn State University at Harrisburg, St. Francis Xavier University, University of New Brunswick, and Brock University in Canada (where she founded and directed the Instructional Development Office). Prior to that she was on Faculty at McGill University from 1976 to 1986.

Chapter 1
Theoretical Framework

• • • • • •

I well remember my initial experiences in teaching adults. I had almost no idea how to plan instruction and, in addition, had been assigned courses in subjects in which I had minimal expertise. So I did what many of us do in such situations: I read the textbook ahead of the students and proceeded to "explain" it in class. When I first tried to introduce group work, after hearing my colleagues talk about it, I simply asked students to discuss a topic from the textbook. When my students began to tell anecdotes about their own experiences during class, I became quite nervous. I thought we were "off track" and that I should get things back "under control." Nevertheless, I was amazed at the energy generated by people talking to each other in the classroom. It also seemed right that these people, experienced teachers themselves, should be able to talk about their practice. Later, I agonized over the first set of grades I gave. Were they too high? Too low? Would my colleagues think I was a pushover? Would my students think I was unfair?

Even those of us who studied adult education before teaching our first course or giving our first workshop probably can recount similar stories. Learning to teach not only grows out of abstract study, but also out of practical experience and reflection on that experience over time. Ideally, we read about teaching, think about it, discuss with colleagues, try it out in our own practice, adjust it, read some more, try it out again, and eventually find our own style and way of being a teacher.

Yet, I believe there are some fundamentals of planning instruction and working with learners that can act as a guide for all educators.

Without these, we can flounder around unnecessarily for a long time. For example, several years passed before I realized that different teaching strategies were appropriate for different kinds of knowledge. I have also seen experienced educators who evaluate learning with multiple-choice tests even though their goal is to encourage critical thinking. I still hear teachers say that time constraints and curriculum load prevents them from allowing their students to discuss issues in class or to engage in independent learning projects. Without an understanding of the fundamental decisions that must be made in educational practice and knowledge of the basis on which to make these decisions, teaching is indeed an overwhelming enterprise.

In this chapter, I introduce the concept of planning instruction in adult education. I then provide an overview of some theoretical frameworks that can inform us about our decision making and planning in our practice.

Planning Instruction in Adult Education

Traditional instructional design is defined as the systematic planning of instruction and includes considering the characteristics of learners, setting objectives, sequencing instruction, selecting instructional strategies (methods and materials), evaluating learning, and evaluating instruction.

Within adult education today, theorists and practitioners more commonly talk about program planning rather than instructional design. Sork (2010) describes the contemporary understandings of program planning and examines some of the alternatives to the traditional step-by-step linear approaches. The traditional approach has a foundation of technical rationality, leading to predictable outcomes, although some planners, such Cervero and Wilson (2006) consider the negotiation of power to be central to the planning process. Interactive and question-based approaches to planning have also come to our attention. Caffarella (2002) proposes an interactive model that contains twelve components, some of which sound like traditional planning steps (for example, developing objectives, designing instructional plans, formulating evaluation plans) and others of which are based on communication and interaction (for example, building support, prioritizing program ideas, making recommendations and communicating results, coordinating facilities). Similarly, Sork and Newman (2004) emphasize using a series of questions related to common elements of planning, those elements also being similar to the step-by-step models (for example, analyzing the context and the learner group, clarifying intentions, preparing instructional plans, developing evaluation plans).

The seeming conflict between instructional design or planning and adult education comes from planning models that are instrumental in nature (taking a technical approach to learning and teaching) and theoretical approaches to adult education that advocate empowerment and emphasize communicative and emancipatory learning. However, as Sork (2010) says, "But this isn't an argument to reject technical rationality completely as a part of effective practice …only as the *exclusive* basis for taking practical action" (p. 161).

The conceptual framework of systematic planning remains valuable. No matter what or where we teach, we do need to know what it is people want to learn, create a sequence or structure for working toward that learning, help learners find appropriate and effective learning strategies and experiences, and include reliable ways of knowing if and when learning occurs.

Educators worry that systematic instructional planning may eliminate the art of education and interfere with creativity and flexibility. We want to be conscious of diversity among learners, the emotional and spiritual aspects of learning, and holistic approaches to learning. However, this does not prevent us from taking what is useful from instructional design procedures and incorporating this into our own beliefs, values, and approaches to education. Educational research has demonstrated that the teaching and learning process is a complex interaction among students, teacher, cultural and political issues, experience, environment, and the subject under study. But we also know that students need to articulate their learning goals, connect their learning to their experience, and enjoy the activities they engage in. Through an informed planning process, we can do our best to ensure that these features exist in our teaching and learning practice.

The adult education literature tells us that adult learners are or want to be self-directed; that is, they know what they want to learn and have a good idea of how best they learn. The educator is a facilitator who guides, supports, and challenges rather than directs and prescribes. Group work, discourse with others, and the exchange of experiences among learners is an essential part of meaningful learning. Students can learn to evaluate their own work. Does this free us of the responsibility to plan? We may be more in need of planning than ever, if we hope to orchestrate such a complex process. My classroom may look messy to an outside observer, but the messiness is well planned.

We all have experience with and habits of mind about what a teacher's role is. The teachers many of us have known always stood at the front of the room, told us what to do, and gave out grades. To plan instruction does not imply that we ignore the personalities and learning styles of our students or their backgrounds and experiences. Nor does it suggest that we should not let them talk to each other or that we should threaten and intimidate them with our power. And, in particular, planning does not stifle flexibility, creativity, innovation, or intuitive hunches in our practice. Good planning fosters good learning.

In the adult education context, objectives can be developed for, with, or by adult learners. Ordering or sequencing learning experiences can be determined for or with the students, depending on their prior knowledge of the subject area. The selection of instructional strategies can be based on the preferences and needs of the learners, and we can expect them to participate in and contribute to the development and design of learning activities. The most exciting classroom projects are often those facilitated by learners in the group. Evaluation of learning is sometimes informal, sometimes formal, but students always can be actively involved in the process, whether through self-evaluation strategies, constructing test items, or setting criteria. Of course, student involvement in the evaluation of instruction is essential; only they can judge how well it is working for them.

A wide variety of adult education activities and settings exist, from community action networks to self-help groups, from professional development workshops to recreational instruction, from adult basic education courses to college and university programs. The workshop leader of a session on teamwork in the workplace will have quite different concerns from the person who is training apprentice mechanics. The facilitator of a course on small business operations in a community development program sees his practice as distinct from that of his colleague who teaches in the Faculty of Management at a nearby university. The workshop leader and the community development facilitator do not give tests nor assign grades. The workshop leader may see her participants only once. The mechanics instructor may work intensively with his students over several months or a year. The university professor may not concern herself with students' prior learning if they have taken a prerequisite course. Despite this diversity of practice, I nevertheless believe that, to be effective, each of us must know something about our students, determine our goals, order the topics we present, employ sound teaching methods and materials, be able to judge if and when our students or participants learn something, and determine whether or not we are doing a good job. In other words, the components of the instructional design model are relevant regardless of the context within which we work.

Theoretical Foundations of Adult Education

Merriam and Brockett (2007) define adult education as "activities intentionally designed for the purpose of bringing about learning among those whose age, social roles, or self perception define them as adults." (p. 8) Merriam and Brockett see the notion of adulthood as a stage of life as a relatively new concept. Legal definitions of adulthood tend to be based on age, but most definitions of adulthood are culturally and socially constructed. Hansman and Mott (2010) consider various facets of what makes up adulthood and come to the following definition: "persons may be considered adults when they have taken on the social, psychological, and/or economic roles typically expected of adults in their cultures and collective societies" (p. 14).

As an area of academic investigation, adult education is relatively new. Although adult education has taken place in some form throughout history, professional preparation of adult educators at colleges or universities has occurred only in the last few decades. Since theoretical development of a field is, to a large extent, dependent on it existing at universities with graduate studies, the theoretical foundations of adult education have been flourishing in the last 35 years or so (if we think of Malcolm Knowles as a starting point of the flourishing period).

A theory is simply an explanation of the relationship among facts or observations with a goal of predicting future events. If an instructor was to observe, for example, that standing over and shouting at individuals in his group seemed to cause them to cringe, cover their ears, and eventually become quite anxious and fearful, he might develop a theory that loud noises increase anxiety. This theory could be tested further, other factors could be considered to make sure that it really was the loud noise that caused the apprehension. The theory is the explanation of the relationship between the two behaviors—shouting and cringing.

Theories are developed in two ways. Someone may have an idea or a "hunch" as to how things are related, then collect information to prove or disprove that hunch. Or, someone may collect data and from these data develop an explanation. Most theories are developed slowly and carefully over many years.

In the arena of teaching and learning we cannot apply methods taken from the sciences. Learning cannot be measured using a caliper; counting the number of times a specific behavior happens cannot explain teaching. Knowledge about teaching and learning is not technical and predictable as is knowledge about mathematics or science. Rather, it is based on people's perceptions of what happens, how people communicate with each other, and on our understanding of social expectations and norms. The teacher who inspires me may leave you cold. The teacher who works well with small groups of tradespeople may be at a loss giving an academic lecture. There are no absolute or objective truths to be discovered.

As long as we accept their limitations and continue to question their validity in our context, theories can provide us with ways of summarizing, explaining, interpreting, and understanding the multifaceted nature of our practice. A theory can offer us guidelines, suggestions, or new ideas for our work with learners. If, for example, I accept a theory that people become more open to alternatives when they have the opportunity to engage in critical reflection, I may decide to incorporate strategies that encourage reflection, such as journal writing, in my course. Although theories of teaching and learning cannot provide us with clear predictions, they remain important for educators who are interested in developing their practice.

It is difficult to separate theories of instruction from theories of learning. There is no instruction without learning, or at least without learners. There may, however, be learning without teaching. The separation I make here is open to critical questioning. Those theories I present as theories of instruction focus on what the educator does, though this, of course, is in the context of promoting and understanding learning. Those theories I present as theories of learning emphasize the process of learning, usually with clear implications for teaching. For more detailed descriptions of theoretical approaches, I recommend Merriam and Brockett (2007), Kasworm, Rose, and Ross-Gordon (2010), and Merriam, Caffarella, and Baumgartner (2007).

Theories of Instruction

Interest in theories of instruction was much more common in the past than it is today. In the early 1900s, educational researchers focused a great deal of attention on trying to determine which teaching methods were most effective, and theorists struggled to articulate general models of good education. But beginning in the late 1950s, this work was critiqued. In his then much-quoted address to the American Psychological Association in 1957, Lee Cronbach suggested that no one method would ever prove to be more effective than another since individual learners reacted in different ways to each method. For some time, theorists then concentrated on trying to understand how we learn as a way of informing teaching models. Theories and models of instruction remain valuable in stimulating reflection on our practice.

John Dewey Many of the current approaches to adult education can be traced directly to the writings of John Dewey (1916, 1938), even though his work did not deal exclusively with teaching adults. Dewey portrayed education as a lifelong process. He proposed that we learn by experience, a radical thought at that time. In experiential learning, a person faces a series of problems to be solved and approaches them using a process similar to the scientific method; that is, he or she develops hypotheses about these problems and collects evidence to confirm or deny the hypotheses. Another key component of Dewey's conceptualization of learning was reflection—the means by which we assess the basis for our beliefs. These two concepts—learning by experience and reflection—remain integral elements of modern-day descriptions of adult education. To approach learning in this way leads to a model of instruction in which the teacher's role is one of guide and facilitator rather than expert or formal authority.

- The educator selects experiences for and with the learner.
- The learner's needs and past experiences are an integral part of the teaching and learning process.
- Students participate in cooperative and mutual learning experiences with the teacher.
- The environment must be considered in all learning experiences.

Eduard Lindeman In 1926, Eduard Lindeman wrote the first book on adult education, *The Meaning of Adult Education*. With the publication of this book, followed by the founding of the American Association for Adult Education, professional literature on adult education came into being. In the 1920s, 1930s, and 1940s, Lindeman dedicated himself to the development of democratic values in adult education. He believed that working toward a democratic process involved critical analysis, concern for others, the acceptance of opposing perspectives, and a willingness to live with potentially uncomfortable majority decisions. It is, in Lindeman's view, the overarching goal of adult education to foster the democratic process. Thus, he insisted that adult education was more than just a technical practice and strongly advocated its social purpose.

Lindeman agonized over if and how educators should impose their beliefs on others when teaching, and when and how educators should withdraw from learning groups as they became empowered.

- Adult education is an act of free will.

- Discussion or discourse is the primary teaching method.

- The goal of adult education is a democratic society informed by networks of discussion groups.

Paulo Freire   Like Lindeman, Paulo Freire (1973), who worked in Brazil with oppressed and illiterate people, held that social change was the goal of teaching adults. Through his work, Freire recognized that illiteracy results in a power imbalance. He believed that the "banking model" of teaching (depositing knowledge in an empty mind) simply reinforces the notion that the teacher has the power (the knowledge) and does nothing to empower the students. He advocated that educators become co-learners, working with people, taking part in their culture. In his Pedagogy of Hope (Freire, 1994), he explores the same themes, but with the added power that comes from his decades of work as a teacher. He argues that "educational practice, whether it be authoritarian or democratic, is always directive" (p. 79). The moment this direction interferes with the learner's own capacity to learn, it becomes manipulative. Education is political and directive, never neutral, and must always respect opposing positions. The role of the educator is to understand and become a part of the learner's culture, to stimulate learning, and hence to free or empower the individual.

- The educator is also a learner, listening to and understanding the needs and culture of the individual.

- Learners participate actively in the learning process, through dialogue with their teacher, who is a co-learner with them.

- Educator and learners are mutually responsible for the teaching and learning process.

Malcolm Knowles I think it is safe to say that no name is as eminent in the field of adult education as that of Malcolm Knowles. His writing guided teachers, researchers, and theorists for decades (for example, see Knowles, 1978, 1980, 1984). He popularized the term "andragogy," defining it as the "art and science of helping adults learn" (Knowles 1980, p. 30). In his typically modest and gentle fashion, he later wrote, "andragogy is simply another model of assumptions about learners to be used alongside the pedagogical model of assumptions" (Knowles 1980, p. 43). Malcolm Knowles had a vision, one that stayed with him throughout his prolific career and served as the driving force behind innumerable courses, programs, and institutions across North America. He introduced us to learning contracts. He advocated self-directed learning. He encouraged us to work with students to achieve their own learning goals rather than to tell them what to learn and how to learn it.

In 1991, he described his dream:

> A panoramic vision of the entire field of adult learning (notice the dropping of the term education from the field's name), worldwide, appears in my dream. The vision is teeming with activity. Groups of adult learners are meeting in all sorts of places, but mostly in places of work, voluntary associations, and lifelong learning centers. By far the largest number of adult learners are in their homes, working alone or with two or three neighbors with multimedia packages....

> Schools and colleges are no longer operating as independent, often competing institutions but are amalgamated into lifelong learning systems, and learning resource centers are located in every community. (p. 449)

He goes on to advocate the replacement of teachers, counselors, and librarians with educational diagnosticians to help people understand what they need to learn, educational planning consultants to help learners design plans to meet their goals, subject specialists, and media specialists.

Knowles' thinking rests on four basic assumptions about the art and science of helping adults learn.

- As a normal aspect of the process of maturation people move from dependency toward increasing self-directedness, but at varying rates and during different stages of life. Teachers have a responsibility to encourage and nurture this movement towards independence. Adults have a deep psychological need to be generally self-directing, although they may be dependent in specific and temporary situations.

- As people grow and develop, they accumulate an increasing reservoir of experience that becomes a rich resource for learning both for themselves and for others. People attach more meaning to the learning gained from experience than to the learning acquired passively. Accordingly, the primary techniques in education are experiential techniques, such as laboratory experiments, discussion, problem-solving cases, simulation exercises, and field experiences.

- People become ready to learn something when they experience a need to learn it in order to cope more effectively with real-life tasks or problems. The educator has a responsibility to create conditions and provide tools and procedures for helping learners discover their "need to know." Learning programs should be organized around life-application categories and sequenced according to the learners' readiness to learn.

- Learners see education as the process of developing increased competence to achieve their full potential in life. They want to be able to apply whatever knowledge and skill they gain today to living more effectively tomorrow. Accordingly, learning experiences should be organized around competency-development categories. People are performance-centered in their orientation to learning.

Based on these assumptions, Knowles and other writers provide detailed instructions for practice and suggestions for research and theory building. Many of the ramifications of Knowles' theory have become commonly accepted practice in adult education.

- The learning climate, both physical and psychological, should be carefully developed. The physical environment should be one in which adults feel at ease, and be informally arranged and decorated, with sufficient light and good acoustics. The psychological environment should be one of acceptance, respect, and support, where freedom of expression exists without fear of punishment or ridicule.

- The adult's desire for self-direction is in direct conflict with the traditional practice of instructor-directed learning. The learner should diagnose learning needs. The instructor should create a model of the competencies or characteristics required to achieve a given ideal model of performance, provide diagnostic experiences in which the learners can assess their present level of competencies in the light of those portrayed in the model, and help learners to measure the gaps between their present competencies and those required by the model (Knowles 1980, pp. 47-48).

- Students should be involved in the planning of their own learning, with the instructor acting as a guide and resource person.

- The teaching and learning process is the mutual responsibility of the instructor and the learner. The instructor's role is one of resource person, co-inquirer, facilitator, catalyst, and guide.

- "Nothing makes an adult feel more childlike than being judged by another adult; it is the ultimate sign of disrespect and dependency, as the one who is being judged experiences it" (Knowles 1980, p. 49). Based on andragogical assumptions, the learner should evaluate her own progress, with the instructor helping to gather evidence as to the extent goals are being reached. Knowles describes evaluation as a re-diagnosis of learning needs.

- Adults are themselves a rich resource of experience. They learn from listening to, analyzing, and questioning each other's experiences. Instructional strategies that take advantage of what students know and have done include discussion, problem-solving exercises, group work, case studies, role-playing, simulations, and field experiences.

- The practical application of learning should be emphasized and related to the lives of students.

- "The appropriate organizing principle for sequences of adult learning is *problem areas*, not *subjects*" (Knowles 1980, p. 54). Adult learners tend to be interested in and ready to solve problems. The starting point for instruction should be the problem or concern that adults have as they enter the educational setting. Subsequent activities can be centered on the problems or tasks arising from the initial needs and diagnoses.

In 1986, Stephen Brookfield's book, *Understanding and Facilitating Adult Learning*, helped adult educators ask constructive critical questions of Knowles' andragogical model. Although Brookfield described adult educators as embracing Knowles' way of understanding our practice, he questioned some of the underlying assumptions of andragogy, especially whether or not adults actually are or can be self-directed. He acknowledged that self-direction and autonomy in work, personal relationships, social structures, and educational pursuits are desirable but perhaps not empirically demonstrated (p. 94). Malcolm Knowles' work, however, gave adult educators a unique identity, an identity which has lingered despite the ways in which we have moved forward in understanding theoretical conceptualizations of educating adults.

In the 1990s, critiques of andragogy continued. Pratt (1993), for example, suggests that andragogy did not live up to our expectations for how it would contribute to the field. Critical theorists, such as Collins (1998), focused on the technical rationality inherent in andragogy (with its black and white or cause and effect statements).

Yet, it seems we still are shaped by Knowles' work, though we no longer cite him except in historical descriptions of the field. Smith (2010) for example, provides an overview of contemporary theories in the facilitation and design of adult learning. She describes a current shift from teacher-centered to learner-centered instruction (as Knowles advocated 30 years ago). Smith believes that this shift has failed due to "an incongruence between espoused theories and theories-in-use" and "the separation of the mind, body, and spirit in learning" (pp. 147-148). In other words, we do not do what we say we are doing, and we do not consider the whole person in planning instruction.

Also in line with earlier theorists, Smith sees adult educators as promoting contextualized learning; that is, learning that is culturally, professionally, and personally relevant, and she notes that approaches to adult education have long had the goal of empowering and liberating learners.

Theories of Learning

Early learning theories were taken from behaviorist and cognitive psychology and from humanistic psychology (Carl Rogers, for example). In Merriam, Caffarella, and Baumgartner's (2007) comprehensive overview of adult learning theories, the authors list Knowles' andragogy, self-directed learning, transformative learning, and experiential learning as classic approaches. Newer approaches include: embodied, spiritual, and narrative learning; non-Western perspectives; and critical theory, postmodern and feminist perspectives. Andragogy has been discussed above as a theory of instruction; in this section, I provide an overview of some of the classic and current theories of learning, specifically self-directed learning, transformative learning, embodied learning, and narrative learning.

Self-directed Learning Self-directed learning has long been a central concept to adult education, yet it is far less evident in practice than in theory, and since the mid 1980s, research and theory development in self-directed learning has diminished considerably. Interest in self-directed learning was first piqued by Alan Tough's (1967) research in which he found that a large majority of adults learn outside of formal educational institutions. Knowles' (1975) book, *Self-Directed Learning*, brought the concept into the forefront of the adult education classroom, especially with the use of learning contracts and clearly defined procedures for encouraging students to formulate and work towards their own learning goals.

The term, "self-directed learning" came to mean several different things over the years. In a comprehensive review of the work on self-directed learning from the 1970s and 1980's, Candy (1991) described four interrelated dimensions.

- *Personal autonomy*, the disposition toward thinking and acting independently in all situations and the inclination to exert control over one's learning endeavors.
- *Self-management*, the willingness and capacity to conduct one's own education.
- *Learner control*, the means by which instruction is organized in formal settings so as to allow students to make decisions about their learning.
- *Autodidaxy*, the individual, non-institutional pursuit of learning opportunities in the natural societal setting.

Merriam, Caffarella and Baumgartner (2007) say that there are three main goals of self-directed learning: to encourage adults to become self-directed, to foster transformative learning through self-directed learning, and to promote emancipatory learning and social action (p. 107). They also suggest that there are three types of models of self-directed learning as a process: linear models (such as Knowles' model), interactive models (in which self-direction is collaborative and in a social milieu), and instructional models. One instructional model that was popular during the 1990s is Grow's (1991) *Staged Self-*

Directed learning model. He proposed that there are four stages a learner goes through in becoming self-directed: dependent learner, interested learner, involved learner, and self-directed learner. For each of these stages, Grow proposed suitable learning activities.

Transformative Learning

Over the past three decades, transformative learning theory has become a powerful way of understanding how adults change their beliefs, values, and perspectives. In the mid-seventies, Jack Mezirow's interest in this process was stimulated by the experiences of his wife upon returning to school. He went on to conduct a national study of re-entry college women and identify the patterns of change they went through. Based on this work, Mezirow (1977, 1981) proposed that an individual learns when her perception of reality is "not in harmony with" experience. During a life "crisis" or dilemma (divorce, loss of job, promotion, relocation), people experience disharmony and are receptive to learning. Mezirow (1981) describes a ten-step learning cycle, including:

- A disorienting dilemma.
- Self-examination.
- Critical assessment and a sense of alienation.
- Relating discontent to the experiences of others.
- Exploring options for new ways of behaving.
- Building confidence in new ways of behaving.
- Planning a course of action.
- Acquiring knowledge in order to implement plans.
- Experimenting with new roles.
- Reintegration into society.

From this beginning, Mezirow went on to develop a comprehensive theory of adult learning. His 1991 book, *Transformative Dimensions of Adult Learning*, contains the fullest description of the theory, but Mezirow and others have continued to revise and elaborate on the concepts involved in transformative learning in subsequent years.

At the core of Mezirow's perspective on transformative learning theory is critical reflection and critical self-reflection. Many of our beliefs and perspectives have been uncritically assimilated; that is, we have just accepted the ideas of our family, community, or culture, without ever questioning their validity. When students encounter information or have an experience that is discrepant with what they believe, they may be led to question their assumptions, beliefs, or values. People need to understand their experiences, integrate them with what they know, and make them meaningful. We do this continually in order to avoid the threat of chaos. Even a strange noise or a dark shape in the night will lead us to try to place and understand it. A dark shape in the form of an idea, feeling, experience, or insight that is radically different from what we have always held to be true leads us to try to understand, to make meaning out of it. If, in this process, we revise something we had believed in before, and thereby act in a different way based on this revised perspective, transformative learning has occurred.

Starting in the late 1990s, alternative conceptualizations of transformative learning theory flourished. From the beginning, Mezirow's work was criticized as being too cognitive and rational, paying little attention to emotion, imagination, and neglecting the social context of the learning. Over time, a variety of other theorists worked to overcome these perceived deficiencies in the theory. Taylor (2008) summarizes some of these variations, grouping them into seven categories. In the psychoanalytic view of transformative learning individuals come to understand themselves through bringing the unconscious into consciousness, integrating psychic structures of ego, shadow, anima, and animus. The psychodevelopmental perspective focuses on a continuous gradual transformation over the lifespan. Taylor suggests that little attention is paid to the role of context and social change in these perspectives, but in the social-emancipatory version of transformative learning theory, people are constantly "reflecting and acting on the transformation of their world so that it can become a more equitable place for all to live" (p. 8). A planetary view of transformation is based on the interconnectedness of people with the environment, all of nature, and all of humanity, and as such, is not necessarily a learning theory. The goal of transformation is a restructuring of this entire system to create a better world. The final three perspectives that Taylor describes also may not have the characteristics of a learning theory. They are: a neurobiological perspective, based on research that shows the brain changes as we learn; a cultural-spiritual view; and a race-centric view, which focuses on people of African descent.

Embodied Learning

Embodied learning and somatic learning theories describe how we learn through our bodies. As Boucouvalas and Lipson-Lawrence (2010) discuss, this view challenges the notion that mind and body are separate and that it is the mind only that engages in learning. We often experience, for example, anxiety, fear, anger, joy, and happiness as bodily sensations. Freiler (2008) distinguishes between embodied learning and somatic learning. Somatic learning, she suggests, occurs during purposive body-centered movements such as tai chi and yoga, but we could also take this into the realm of our body learning the movements in a variety of physical activities, including sports, operating equipment, and painting or drawing. My fingers, for example, know how to type, without the involvement of my mind. If I am trying to recall how to spell a word, I can type it in order to find the spelling. Many disciplines involve some form of somatic learning.

Freiler uses the terms embodiment and embodied learning to refer to a holistic way of constructing knowledge with the body working in connection with other ways of knowing such as spiritual, affective, and cultural ways of knowing. Engaging in visualization exercises or guided imagery can lead to a deeper understanding than simply "thinking about" something. Images from films, works of art, and photography can touch us in a spiritual, emotional way and, through body learning, help us to interpret racism, sexism, and classism. Images from Brokeback Mountain, for example, dramatically deepened my understanding of heterosexism. As Freiler says, embodied learning is hard to articulate; it seems to be independent of the words we have available to describe learning. She concludes that it is "a way to construct knowledge through direct engagement in bodily experiences and inhabiting one's body through a felt sense of being-in-the-world" (p. 40), or, more simply, it "involves being attentive to the body and its experience as a way of knowing" (p. 40).

Narrative Learning

Storytelling has long been used in education in all disciplines. It can be as simple as sharing an anecdote with students about our own experience and asking students to do the same, or it can be a structured and planned set of activities designed to engage learners in learning through narrative. The work of Carolyn Clark and Marsha Rossiter (Clark and Rossiter, 2008; Rossiter and Clark, 2007) has brought narrative learning theory into adult education. Clark and Rossiter (2008) suggest that understanding our experiences is a narrative process; this can be done through making connections among our experiences, or by creating a narrative that helps us understand something we are going through, such as an illness or the death of a family member. People tell stories at funerals in order to understand the person's life and death. Narratives are also used to create our sense of self, our identity and our place in the world (family, community, culture). We often have multiple and sometimes contradictory narratives that describe who we are in different contexts. My narrative of being a teacher may be quite different than my narrative of being a mother or a sister.

Randall (1996) writes about using narrative to understand changes in our lives. When a life narrative no longer seems to apply to who we are we "restory" ourselves, create a new narrative that reflects how we have changed or transformed. Clark and Rossiter (2008) also describe a narrative approach to lifespan development and say that the "construction of an acceptable life narrative is the central process of adult development" (p. 62).

We learn through stories in at least three different ways (Clark and Rossiter, 2008): hearing stories, telling stories, and recognizing stories. Hearing others' stories (or reading stories) engages our imagination and emotions as well as our cognition, and can take us to learning from experiences we have not had ourselves. Telling stories and having someone listen carefully to stories allows us to see patterns in our experiences and perhaps imagine how our experiences look from someone else's perspective. Recognizing stories involves positioning ourselves in and seeing a larger context and a larger narrative. As a Canadian currently living in the US, I can see differences in the "Canadian story" and the "US story." As a person living in a rural community where the farm life is giving away to big houses and commuters, I can position myself in that context and question the story that is unfolding.

Some theorists distinguish between narratives and stories (for example, Boje, 2008). Stories are the rather messy first-time tellings of an experience. When stories are repeated, they become more organized and perhaps stylized and are then referred to as narratives. Or when a story is told to someone who then restructures it and tells it for a different purpose (as in narrative research) it becomes a narrative. Here, I use story and narrative interchangeably, as do Clark and Rossiter.

Narrative learning can be fostered in many different ways, for example: reading fiction, watching movies, writing stories, keeping journals, writing autobiographies, describing critical incidents, and using case studies.

Summary

How we plan instruction is informed by what we know about teaching and learning. We choose topics, decide to put them in a specific order, select materials, and design learning activities in an effort to foster learning. Many times we simply base these decisions on previous experience—what worked last time, what we ourselves enjoy as learners, what we have seen a colleague do. We can also draw inspiration from the thinking, writing, and research done by people who dedicate their professional lives to understanding teaching and learning. In this chapter, I bring together some of that work to help us in making good decisions about our practice.

Instructional design is a systematic planning model that leads us through a procedure of considering our learners, setting objectives, ordering topics, selecting methods and materials, and evaluating learning and teaching. Planning does not have to be rigid nor directed in an authoritarian manner by the instructor. It can be open and flexible. It certainly can involve learners in decision making.

Over the past decades, theorists have worked to understand how we can best teach adults. John Dewey tells us that we learn from experience; we learn by doing. Eduard Lindeman reminds us of the social purpose of adult education. Paulo Freire says that we must truly come to know our learners, live in their world and culture, and work with them as co-learners to create knowledge rather than try to deposit knowledge in their empty minds. Malcolm Knowles stresses that people have rich experiences of their own, prefer to direct their own learning, and are interested in solving problems relevant to their lives. Stephen Brookfield adds that we must not only give people what they think they need, but also challenge them to go beyond their expressed needs. And perhaps, he points out, not everyone is as self-directed as we think they should be.

Learning theories take behaviorist, cognitive, humanist, or critical approaches. I provide a brief overview of a few theories (classic and modern) that provide a framework for teaching adults. Self-directed has been a central driving force in the literature on adult learning. Jack Mezirow draws from several diverse areas of study to create a theory of transformative learning, a way of describing how adults change their assumptions, beliefs, values, and perspectives as they go about making meaning out of their experiences in the world. Several authors have elaborated on transformative learning theory to make it more inclusive of imagination, emotions, and social change.

I introduce two newer theoretical approaches: embodied learning (learning through and with our bodies) and narrative learning (learning through telling, hearing, and recognizing stories).

In designing our next workshop, class, course, or program, we can use these ideas to help us make wise and informed decisions about our instruction: decisions based on our own experience, the procedures involved in planning instructions, and the theoretical frameworks that provide a foundation for adult education.

Chapter 2

Considering the Learners

• • • • • •

In every class, workshop, or seminar, we intuitively size up our learners and make decisions about how to proceed based on what we see. And we carry on this process continuously throughout the learning experience, often with little deliberate or conscious thought. Who are these people? How diverse is the group? Are they experts or neophytes? Interested or bored? According to who our learners are and what we perceive their reactions and responses to be, we adjust, change direction, elaborate, give an example, direct, withdraw, and revise. Imagine teaching tennis to first-year undergraduate students in a physical education course. Then imagine teaching tennis to the following: students whose first language is Chinese, corporate executives, Inuit adults, your best friend's spouse, Olympic class swimmers, or young adults in wheelchairs. The whole picture changes and so do our instructional plans.

Ideally we would prefer to discover as much as possible about our learners before starting to teach them, but this is not usually possible. While we may have some general knowledge about our students' professional backgrounds, previous courses or programs, and reasons for enrolment, we rarely have such specific information as their learning styles, past experiences, or what they actually remember from prior courses. Hopefully, we have the opportunity to learn these things as we work with our students.

To begin the planning process, all models include some process whereby we get to know the learners—their characteristics, preferences, and backgrounds. In some circumstances, information is collected in advance directly from learners through questionnaires or tests. Detailed information on educational background, knowledge and skills, age, academic achievement, reading ability, and specific learning needs can be gathered to provide a basis upon which to plan instruction. Sometimes audience analysis is both feasible and desirable. If, for example, we are planning a training program for the staff of an organization, developing modules for use in a specific setting, or preparing a workshop for members of a professional association, we may well be able to carry out such an analysis.

In most adult education settings, however, we do not have the opportunity to do this, or perhaps more importantly, we choose not to do it in order to avoid an intimidating and potentially threatening beginning to the learning experience. As an alternative, Jane Vella (2002) suggests that we get to know our learners by *listening* to them, not questioning them or testing them.

In this chapter, I review some important characteristics of adult learners to consider when planning instruction. Some of these characteristics we may know about in advance, and others we will learn about as we go. Initial plans can and should be modified as we gain further knowledge about our participants. Even in a short workshop, it is reasonable to drop or add an agenda item if the group has more or less expertise or interest in an area than we expected.

In the following discussion I first present some general characteristics of adult learners. Next, I comment on diversity in groups based on experience, education, values, culture, and gender. Third, I discuss learning styles, multiple intelligences, and psychological type preferences. Finally, I provide a brief overview of one approach to adult development.

General Characteristics of Adult Learners

Most standard adult education texts contain information on the characteristics of adult learners (for example, Merriam, Caffarella, and Baumgartner, 2007). Dorothy MacKeracher (2004) also provides a comprehensive and interesting discussion of general characteristics, such as past experience, as well as the emotional, cognitive, social, physical, and spiritual aspects of adult learning.

In general, the literature agrees that:

- Most often, adults become involved in a learning situation by choice. When they have chosen to learn, they have clear, specific goals, whether to improve job skills, move up the salary scale, satisfy intellectual curiosity, or make social contacts. They expect the instructional situation to be relevant to them.

- Most adults have concrete, immediate goals. They have taken a course or attended a workshop in order to learn a specific skill or have a certain set of questions addressed.

- Adults may prefer to learn quickly and get on with their lives. Thus, they can be reluctant to become involved in activities and exercises not clearly applicable to their goals.

- Adults enter a learning situation with a variety of life experiences. The older the learners, the more experience they bring and the more varied it will be in any one group. Learning is facilitated when the instruction is related to these experiences.

- Past experience becomes increasingly important in either helping or hindering the learning process as age increases.

- Adults with a positive self-concept will find learning easier. Sometimes, the school setting or any instructional situation is perceived as threatening and has a negative effect on self-concept. Both the instructor and the environment must be supportive and understanding.

- Usually, adults prefer to be self-directed learners. They do not want to be treated like children and told what to do. Since they have their own goals and experiences, they want to find activities and ways of doing things that relate to them. By now, they have established individual preferences for working alone or in groups, and for learning by listening, reading, or doing.

- Some adults in a new learning situation or those returning to school after many years may be anxious or uncomfortable and may demonstrate dependent behaviors. Therefore, introducing self-directed learning may increase their anxiety and discomfort. The role of the educator is then to gradually foster independence and self-direction.

- Adult learning tends to involve transforming knowledge rather than forming new knowledge. This process requires energy, time, trust, and openness.

- Adults are reluctant to change their values, opinions, or behaviors.

Diversity in Adult Learning Groups

Diversity in adult education is most often discussed in relation to race, class and gender (Merriam, Caffarella, and Baumgartner, 2007), as these are contributors to power imbalances and oppression. They are not, though, the only sources of power-based relationships nor are they the only ways in which we understand diversity in learning groups. Whenever one group silences an individual or another group through the use or abuse of power, we need to work toward inclusion of all in our work as educators. This is why diversity needs to be considered in planning instruction. Brookfield (2005), in his comprehensive overview of critical theory, outlines seven learning tasks: (1) challenging ideologies—the ideologies embedded in language, social habits, and cultural forms; (2) contesting hegemony—our acceptance of injustice as being in our own best interests; (3) unmasking power—becoming conscious of power relations; (4) overcoming alienation, which is a product of being unable to be authentic in the way we live and work; (5) learning liberation as a way of escaping one-dimensional thought and ideological; (6) reclaiming reason as a part of moral issues, values, and interpersonal relations, and (7) practicing democracy through rational discourse and paying attention to power structures related to diversity.

Smith (2010) refers to diversity in relation to age, gender, race, sexual-orientation, culture, work experiences, educational background, learning styles, and beliefs about learning and knowledge. She sees a shift to more learner-centered teaching as one way to respond to diversity in our planning of instruction, along with promoting learning that is culturally, professionally, and personally relevant. In the next sections, I discuss diversity in relation to experience, educational background, values, culture (including language), and gender.

Experience Adults may have learned about a subject in a variety of informal ways—for example, becoming familiar with a language by living in a foreign country, acquiring a skill on the job, picking up information about medicine by talking with physician friends, learning about teaching by being a student, studying auto mechanics by repairing their own cars, or exploring the Internet on their home computers. While people may have a good working knowledge of a subject because of extensive prior experience, they may have surface familiarity with, but not necessarily organized knowledge about, a subject. But, experience gained in a practical setting or life situation is valuable and meaningful and needs to be recognized. Educators who minimize learners' sharing of their knowledge are silencing them and excluding them.

In addition, the life experiences of adult learners, whether or not directly related to course content, are equally important for the educator to recognize. In her doctoral dissertation, Barbara Smith (1999) found that one of the primary concerns of older adults in higher education settings was that their professors did not take into account their life experiences. For example, individuals studying history were actually penalized for using their personal experience as a way of understanding historical events through which they had lived. We must not overlook learners' personal knowledge of social and family relationships, organizational and management skills acquired through running a household, self-awareness developed through introspection, or understanding of art, music and literature gained through participation in community agencies.

How do we find out about learners' experience? In a recent course for college teachers, I observed one of the participants, a former tradesperson, as he struggled with the academic content of many of the readings, activities, and discussions. He was older than the rest of the group and made self-derisive comments and jokes about his age on a daily basis. When he participated, he seemed able to do so only by first belittling his own experience. In searching for ways to bring out his experience and help him make it relevant to his learning, I found help in Barbara Smith's (1999) dissertation, which pointed out what this student might be feeling, and the stories in Jane Vella's (2002) *Learning to Listen, Learning to Teach*. After taking the time to meet individually with this student over the weeks, asking him about himself and his life, and listening to what he said, he finally began to value his experience and integrate it into class discussions.

We can bring out and make use of learners' experiences in a variety of informal ways.

- Provide small group activities in which students share experiences relevant to the topic under discussion.

- Encourage students to offer anecdotes as examples and illustrations of points which then can be analyzed and related back to the topic.

- In learning projects, encourage participants to include their own experience.

- Ask students with more experience in an area to teach or show others who have less experience.

- Suggest learners keep journals or diaries in which they relate what they are studying to their own experience.

Educational Background

A person's educational background is relevant to planning instruction for at least three reasons. First, information about the level, duration, content, and quality of their formal education tells us quite a bit about what learners already may know about the subject we are teaching. Second, the nature of their formal education tells us something about their expectations of their current educational experience. For example, students who have taken only teacher-directed courses usually expect a similar approach and may be disconcerted by alternative strategies. Third, knowing when learners were last involved in formal education or how long they have been "out of school" alerts us to the possibility that they may be experiencing anxiety, apprehension, or insecurity, as well as indicating how rusty their reading, writing, and study skills may be.

If a learner has prior knowledge of a subject area, we can continue to build on what people already know, so it can be helpful to ask about prior learning related to the topic of our course, workshop, or program. In some situations, formal assessments of prior knowledge are required—entry examinations for professional training, for example. However, I do not recommend testing adult learners at the beginning of a course or workshop. The negative effect of the anxiety produced outweighs the benefits of having such results. In a workshop for college and university faculty, I handed out a personality inventory as almost the first activity of the session. Even among these seasoned educators, this package produced considerable agitation. "What is this? A test?" they asked. Informally asking learners about their knowledge of a topic or simply observing and listening during discussions is a better approach.

The more basic the level of learner knowledge in a content area, the more effective it is to use methods and materials that provide concrete experience and examples. If the level of knowledge is more advanced and sophisticated, or as it becomes so, more abstract methods and materials may be more appropriate (see Chapters Five and Six).

Examining students' past academic achievement can have mixed results. In a heterogeneous group of people with varied levels of education, this information can help us reach all levels, using a variety of methods and materials. But this knowledge also can easily lead us to develop expectations, which can influence our perception of students and, in turn, influence their learning. Sometimes a colleague tells me a "weak" student is coming into my class, and I need to be careful not to see him or her through someone else's eyes. Sometimes, knowing about our learners' achievement is helpful in planning more effectively, but more often than not, it is probably better not to have or pay attention to this information.

I recommend spending some time, not necessarily very much, informally exploring students' educational backgrounds. How long have they been out of school? What did their previous educational experiences consist of? What specific subjects have they taken? How far did they go in school? Did they like or dislike school? Such background information can be obtained in an introductory icebreaker, a small group activity, or casual group discussion, and can be valuable in gaining some understanding of students' emotional and personal responses, as well as some knowledge of their learning and study skills.

Values There is diversity in every group in relation to the values people hold. Values are often formed early in life and as such are uncritically assimilated; that is, people take on the values of their family, community, and culture without thought. Later in life, people may come to question their values, as they engage in transformative learning, but even so, it is not common to change one's values easily or quickly. Values may be rooted in religious beliefs or in spiritual experiences (Tisdell, 2008). People feel strongly about their values and have an emotional investment in them, so questioning, challenging, or disregarding someone's values is problematic. At the same time, if we are working toward helping people develop more open, permeable, and justified perspectives (based on transformative learning theory), challenge is an integral part of that process.

Depending on the areas in which we teach, different types of values may be relevant. Educators working in training for the trades, for example, may not find religious or spiritual values relevant to their interactions with learners, but they may be more conscious of values related to work ethics or professionalism. Every educator wants his or her learners to come to value the subject area they are teaching, regardless of what it is. When I teach a course on research to teachers who do not see themselves as having any interest in or use for educational research, I try to help them see that all teachers are researchers in their classrooms, and to value that facet of their work.

Mezirow (2000) writes about perspectives related to psychological, sociolinguistic, epistemic, moral-ethical, philosophical, and aesthetic habits of mind. In each of these areas, individuals hold values and make assumptions about what they believe to be true. I might, for example, value independence and autonomy (psychological), hard work (sociolinguistic), collaborative learning (epistemic), the essential goodness of humanity (moral-ethical), a vegan lifestyle (philosophical), and modern art (aesthetic).

Simple activities can be used to help people articulate their values. For example, asking learners to list ten cherished values, then consider how they came to hold those values, and why the value remains important can be revealing for learners and the educator (Cranton, 2001). Taken further, learners can work in pairs to look for patterns in their values (are they primarily related to family, to work, to culture?).

Culture Working with cultural diversity is complex and difficult in that we, too, as educators, are looking through our cultural lens, and cannot have an objective or value-free view. Tisdell (2007) and English and Tisdell (2010) promote culturally responsive teaching through a spiritual lens. Based on her research with 31 adult educators, Tisdell describes culturally responsive teaching occurring through four ways: (1) dealing with internalized oppression and regaining cultural identity, (2) mediating among multiple identities (race, gender, class, sexuality), (3) crossing culture to facilitate spiritual and overall development of a more authentic identity, and (4) exploring unconscious knowledge construction through images, symbols, rituals, and metaphors which are culturally based (English and Tisdell, 2010, pp. 290-291).

Fenwick (2003) explores diversity in connection with experiential learning. She points out that multiculturalism seeks to express different cultural forms without questioning the power relations inherent in that labelling. Labels such as "at-risk, low-income, working class, and ethnic references (i.e., Italian-American, Chinese-Canadian) obscure the complex and often contradictory learning experiences of individuals who live multiple and often hybrid identities across many cultural affiliations" (p. 60). Western models of learning tend to emphasize rationality, autonomy, and independence. Self-directed learning, as described in Chapter 1, is an example of a Western perspective on learning. Other cultures may experience learning that is more holistic, more collaborative, more emotional, and centered on the collective or the community rather than the individual. Lin (2006) focuses on Chinese culture in her discussion of cultural dimensions of authenticity in teaching. She interviewed 15 individuals from China who were studying as graduate students in U.S. universities. One example illustrates a theme in Lin's exploration of this issue. A student described a professor who was teaching drama. He "purchased and wore silk Chinese traditional clothes to make him look like he likes the culture he was teaching within...he was not an authentic teacher to his students or the department he worked for" (p. 65). Lin goes on to say that Chinese values emphasize humility and altruistic behavior, taking the middle path, and listening when conflict arises, values that she sees as opposing the Western view of authentic teaching. Likely this instructor was trying to relate to his learners, but he actually antagonized them by not being aware of cultural values.

In order to begin to understand culture and identity in learning, Fenwick (2003) suggests that we question the assumptions underlying our practice:

- What norms of learning and education are apparent in our practice that potentially repress individuals?

- How do these norms potentially marginalize or distort the perspectives of particular people?

- What experiences of oppression are rendered invisible by our teaching materials and strategies?

- In what ways to we presume sameness among people?

- Who enjoys unacknowledged privilege in the methods we use?

- What knowledge counts most in what we emphasize and reward?

- What knowledge is undervalued in our practice? (pp. 61-62)

Gender When gender is discussed in relation to diversity, it is usually the overlap between several aspects of diversity that is of interest; for example, how gender, race, sexual orientation, and class interact (Hart, 2005). A social justice orientation to adult education is focused on understanding how oppression occurs and how we need to work toward equality while honoring diversity.

Gender has also been discussed in relation to learning style and "ways of knowing." Carol Gilligan (1986), a pioneer in the study of women's development, argues that while the identity of boys is built on separation from their primary female caregiver, girls develop their sense of self through the sameness and attachment to their primary caregiver. Males value separateness, autonomy, and independence;

females value relationships and responsibilities, empathy, and interdependence. In a review of several studies, Caffarella and Olson (1993) found support for Gilligan's work. Interpersonal relationships were found to be central to women's self-concept. Women's development tends to be diverse and nonlinear, changing with the variety of roles they assume. MacKeracher (2004) discusses relational learning strategies—those that emphasize collective and collaborative group activities, learning partnerships, and a holistic cognitive style—and suggests that although some men prefer relational strategies and some women prefer autonomous strategies, women more often than men engage in relational learning.

Brookfield (2010) refers to this literature and points out the debate that followed the work of Belenky, Clinchy, Goldberger, and Tartule. He suggests the dangers of further marginalizing women as learners by labelling them as caring, nurturing, and relational, leaving, by implication, rationality to men. In a society that values rationality over caring, this attempt to recognize the diversity inherent in gender may oppress women rather than acknowledge differences that need to be addressed in planning instruction

Multiple Intelligences, Emotional Intelligence, and Learning Style

Several different approaches have been taken to understanding individual differences in the acquisition of knowledge and learning preferences. The development of this area in adult learning theory took place largely in the 1980s and 1990s when theorists broke away from the traditional notions of intelligence and began to recognize other ways of learning and knowing.

Howard Gardner's theory of multiple intelligences has remained a popular way of understanding differences among people (Gardner, 1993; Gardner, Kornhaber, and Wake, 1996). Each person's intellect is described as being made up of autonomous faculties that can work individually or in concert with other faculties. Gardner identified eight such faculties, which he labeled as intelligences: musical intelligence, bodily-kinesthetic intelligence, logical-mathematical intelligence, linguistic intelligence, spatial intelligence, interpersonal intelligence, intrapersonal intelligence, and naturalistic.

People may exhibit high intelligence in one or two or more areas and be average in the others. For the educator who thinks that intelligence consists only of the traditional logical and linguistic abilities, Gardner's theory opens up new possibilities of how to approach teaching and learning.

Another interesting approach to understanding intellect came with Goleman's (1998) notion of emotional intelligence. Emotional intelligence includes knowing and managing one's emotions, motivating oneself, recognizing emotions in others, and handling relationships. Empathy, understanding others, and social skills, such as the ability to evoke response in others, are characteristic competencies of emotional intelligence. People high in emotional intelligence, Goleman says, are much more likely to be successful at work. McEnrue and Groves (2006) provide a review of assessments of emotional intelligence for use with adult learners.

Learning styles are preferences for certain conditions or ways of learning. Although we can learn in ways we do not actually prefer, when given a choice, most people have favorite strategies and approaches. MacKeracher (2004) reminds us that learning styles are value-neutral; that is, one style is not better, more productive, or more efficient than another.

Kolb Kolb's (1984) work on learning style and his Learning Style Inventory remains one of the most popular and commonly used ways of understanding learning style after more than two decades. Kolb proposes that we go through a learning cycle of four stages.

- *Concrete experience:* being involved in a new learning situation.
- *Reflective observation:* observing others while they are involved in a new experience or reflecting on our own experience.
- *Abstract conceptualization:* creating concepts and theories to explain our observations.
- *Active experimentation:* using the theories to solve problems and make decisions.

The abilities associated with each of these stages combine to form clusters. People generally prefer one part of the learning cycle over the others, and this defines their learning style.

- *Convergers* prefer abstract conceptualization and active experimentation. They prefer to arrive quickly at specific, concrete solutions. They tend to be unemotional and prefer working with ideas or things rather than people.

- *Assimilators* prefer abstract conceptualization and reflective observation. They like to integrate ideas into models and theories, but are relatively uninterested in the application of the theories in real life.

- *Accommodators* prefer concrete experience and active experimentation. They learn by experience. They adapt well to circumstances and prefer a trial-and-error approach to learning.

- *Divergers* work best in the concrete experience and reflective observation stages of the learning cycle. They generate ideas, are good at brainstorming, and enjoy working with others. However, they do not quickly reach solutions, because they first want to explore all the possibilities in a given situation.

Psychological Type

Psychological type preference models are often listed in discussions of learning style, but they are broader than, say, Kolb's learning style model as they provide an overall integration of traits that describe the nature or unique quality of an individual. Many theorists and researchers have worked to find personality patterns or ways of identifying trends in the psychological and social behavior of humans. I have chosen Carl Jung's ([1921] 1971) theory of psychological type to present here as I see it not only as one of the most comprehensive and still easy-to-understand systems, but also because it is the basis of several popular personality inventories. The Kiersey Temperament Sorter and the Myers-Briggs Type Indicator are two well-known assessments of psychological type preferences. A colleague and I also developed the PET (Personal Empowerment through Type) Check (Cranton and Knoop, 1995; www.learningstyles.ca/HigherEducation).

Jung defines two attitudes toward the world: introversion (a focus on the inner self) and extraversion (a focus on the world outside of the self). He identifies four functions of living: thinking (making logical and analytical judgments), feeling (making judgments based on values), sensing (perceiving through the senses), and intuition (perceiving through hunches and possibilities). The attitudes and functions are combined to make eight psychological types or preferences. Each person has all eight capabilities, but tends to have one as a dominant preference and one as a secondary preference.

- When people use the extraverted thinking function they take concepts and ideas from the world and make judgments about them in a rational and logical manner. Facts and ideals guide their thinking. They have strong principles, are logical and organized, and are interested in truth and justice.

- When introverted thinking is a preference, people's thoughts are generated from within. They enjoy working logically and analytically with theories and models, but are less interested in the practical application of their ideas in the outside world.

- A preference for extraverted feeling means that individuals make judgments based on values and social norms. They adhere to culturally accepted traditions and therefore tend to be in harmony with the world around them and the people in it.

- Introverted feeling is characterized by judgments based on personal or inner values rather than tradition. Values, likes, and dislikes are subjectified or made personal.

- When people use the extraverted sensing function, they use their senses to pay attention to everything in their environment. As a result, they are well adjusted to reality and orient themselves by concrete facts and actual experiences.

- The introverted sensing function interprets the perceptions made through the senses in a subjective manner. Personal significance is added to sensations. Although there is a focus on concrete experience, its meaning is transposed in an inner process.

- When individuals prefer the extraverted intuitive function, they envision things as they could be rather than as they are. They have insights into what is about to happen or how things could develop. Their perceptions are of the future.

- The introverted intuitive functions perceives inner images and seems to be psychic—the images seem to come out of nowhere, although they may be stimulated by something in the environment.

Learning styles clearly can be derived from an understanding of psychological type (Cranton, 2006).

- By using extraverted thinking, a person learns through planning, organizing, and structuring learning experiences.
- With introverted thinking, a learner is reflective, contemplative, and critical.
- Extraverted feeling leads to a preference for collaborative and group learning.
- The use of the introverted feeling function leads to a process of personalizing and internalizing of values during the learning experience.
- When a learner uses extraverted sensing, she learns by doing, experiencing, and engaging in practical activities.
- Introverted sensing is expressed through learning by observing, taking in information with the senses, and attaching personal meaning to it.
- A person who uses extraverted intuition during learning is interested in envisioning possibilities, and engaging in exploratory, unstructured experiences.
- Introverted intuition relies on imagining, following inner images, and working independently.

Developmental Stage

Learners in any adult education setting most probably have progressed to different stages in their personal and professional life. Although our goal as educators is to foster learner development, it is important to recognize that people will occupy different places along any developmental continuum and therefore likely will respond differently to instruction.

Theorists have described the stages of human life in many ways, including moral development, ego development, cognitive development, personality development, and self-actualization. Most developmental frameworks move from a simple, black-and-white understanding of the world to an integrated, more complex perspective. Several decades ago, Erickson's (1959) now-classic work started with a stage of basic trust versus mistrust in infancy and ended with a stage of integrity versus despair in old age. Weathersby's (1981) ego stages include impulsive and self-protective, conformist, self-aware, conscientious, individualistic, and autonomous and integrated stages. Perry's (1999) well-known cognitive development model describes "positions" rather than "stages" and is hierarchical and sequential as were the earlier models. In the first position, knowledge is right or wrong; from there, the person moves through positions of coming to see that knowledge can be relative, ending up in a position where the complexity of knowing one's own beliefs while respecting the knowledge of others.

Similar to those models already mentioned in terms of the general approach, but specifically created to describe adult learning, King and Kitchener (1994) propose seven stages of reflective judgment based on fifteen years of research with adult learners. The first three stages they call pre-reflective thinking, the next two, quasi-reflective thinking, and the final two, reflective thinking. Their model may be one of the most useful for us to consider in planning instruction.

- Stage 1 is characterized by concrete, single-category belief systems. There is an absolute correspondence between what is seen and what is true. Ambiguities do not exist; knowledge is absolute.

- In Stage 2, people believe that there is a true reality that can be known with certainty, but everyone does not know it. Experts and authorities such as teachers, scientists, and religious leaders know the truth. People who disagree with authorities are wrong. Knowledge is absolute, but not immediately available.

- Individuals demonstrating Stage 3 characteristics believe that in some cases even authorities may not currently know the truth. However, the truth will come out—we will discover it. Knowledge is absolutely certain, but can be temporarily uncertain. When the truth is not yet known, a person holds personal beliefs about how it will be.

- In Stage 4 (the beginning of quasi-reflective thinking), people believe that one cannot know with certainty. Knowledge begins to be understood as abstract rather than concrete. Knowledge claims are idiosyncratic and influenced by situational variables. Individuals may argue that they know what is right for themselves, but not for others.

- Stage 5 is set apart by a belief that people know things within a context, based on subjective interpretations of evidence. Knowledge is filtered by the perceptions of the person making the interpretation. Knowing remains context bound: although people at this stage will relate two abstractions (for example, how students learn and how instructors teach), they do not yet relate several abstractions in a system that allows comparisons across contexts.

- Stage 6 is considered as reflective thinking. People argue that knowledge is not a given, but must be constructed. Knowledge is uncertain and must be understood in relationship to context and evidence. Interpretations that are derived from an evaluation of evidence across contexts and the opinions of reputable others are considered as "known."

- In Stage 7, knowledge is the product of reasonable inquiry. It is constructed through critical inquiry and the synthesis of evidence and opinion. Solutions to complex or ambiguous problems are evaluated in terms of what is most reasonable or probable on the basis of current evidence. Knowledge is reevaluated when new evidence, perspectives, or ways of examining the problem are discovered.

King and Kitchener's seven developmental stages are sequential as a person progresses from one to another. They are also closely related to age and educational level.

A somewhat different way of viewing development comes from Kegan's work (Kegan, 2000; Kegan and Lahey, 2009). Kegan's theory is described as a constructive-development theory, meaning that it is concerned with the ways or "form" of knowing ourselves and our surroundings rather than what we know and believe. Kegan describes four plateaus of learning and has several shades of in-between-plateau transitioning.

- Instrumental plateau in which knowledge is tangible, concrete, and obtainable from people who know (this is similar to Perry's first position and King and Kitchener's first stage)

- Socialized plateau in which people follow the values and expectations of others they work with and others with whom they share a community

- Self-authoring plateau in which people construct their own knowledge and values and are not necessarily concerned with others perceptions of them

- Self-transforming plateau in which individuals question the premises of the form of knowing

Summary

This chapter provides an overview of some of the general characteristics of adult learners. Adults come into instructional settings with diverse experiences, values, and cultural backgrounds. These sources of diversity, along with gender, are discussed. I reviewed some of the different ways in which people learn and view knowledge: multiple intelligences, emotional intelligence, learning styles, and psychological type preferences. Although it is not possible (or even desirable) to try to engage every learner using their preferred styles (learning to learn from different approaches is valuable as well), an awareness of these differences goes far in helping us to design activities and sessions that have enough variety to involve most individuals at any one time.

In some settings, it is appropriate to administer a learning style or psychological type inventory, and when this is the case, we should take the time to do so. Not only do we learn how to work better with our students, but also students themselves gain meaningful insights into their own learning.

Adult learners develop over a lifetime, so in any one class, workshop, or training program, there are likely to be people at different places in their development. I end the chapter by reviewing several models of adult development. Although they use a variety of terminology, these models generally describe a developmental process that moves from concrete, authority-based, black-and-white thinking through to complex, constructed ways of knowing that show a tolerance of ambiguity and abstraction.

Chapter 3

Writing Objectives

An objective is a statement of what participants are expected to learn or be able to do after instruction. Just as we have objectives in our daily lives—running five miles a day, spending more time with our children, or delegating some of our work to others—we have objectives for teaching and learning. When we develop a course on homeopathic medicine to add to a program for family physicians, our objective is that this knowledge will be added to the physicians' repertoire. When we select topics or readings for a course, workshop, or training session, we do so on the basis of what we think people should learn. Creating more formal statements of these expectations in the form of objectives is to everyone's advantage.

Whether we write objectives in advance of meeting the students or in collaboration with students, or if students develop their own objectives, the remainder of the instructional process tends to fall into place as objectives are created. We see more clearly and easily which methods will be most appropriate, which materials will be most relevant, and how learning and teaching can best be evaluated.

In this chapter, I first discuss the uses of objectives, how they are of value to instructors, students, and others in the educational setting. I also raise and answer some of the concerns expressed by teachers about the use of objectives. I then give practical guidelines for writing good learning objectives, keeping in mind that learning is open-ended and multi-faceted, including everything from the acquisition of facts and skills to the development of professional or personal value systems. I discuss some of the different ways of classifying learning by using the traditional frameworks of cognitive, affective, and psychomotor learning, while relating these frameworks to alternative conceptualizations of kinds of knowledge such as emotional, relational, and somatic knowing. I give examples of objectives for different kinds of learning. I conclude the chapter by considering some of the ways in which objectives can be used so as not to override adult students' needs to be self-directed and involved in the design of their own learning experiences.

Uses of Objectives

Objectives serve somewhat different purposes for students and instructors and others in educational settings. For students, objectives are useful in several ways.

- Objectives clarify expectations, either the educator's, the students', or both. Most people like to know where they are going. Even when we prefer to meander along, following tangents and exploring ideas, we have that as a goal—we want to explore.

- Objectives act as a guide for focusing attention on relevant points in lectures, discussions, readings, and activities or projects. Being unable to detect the important concepts in a discussion or discern the purpose of an article probably has frustrated all of us at some time. If students know what they want to get out of the educational experience, if they have clear expectations as to the learning goals, they can, for example, re-frame the discussion or find a better article.

- Good objectives can increase motivation. Interesting, tantalizing objectives lead students to look forward to what is coming next. When I participated in a series of workshops on small business operations, I found myself highly motivated by knowing that I would be able to write a marketing plan as one outcome of the learning experience.

- Objectives help students to determine how much they have learned. In a forum that includes testing, this can help individuals see how well prepared they are for an evaluation. Objectives also help people develop self-evaluation skills. When we have something to compare ourselves to—the standard or criterion implicit in an objective—it is much easier to assess learning.

For instructors, objectives are an invaluable aid in both the planning process and throughout the instruction.

- Organizing instruction from class to class or within a workshop or individual session is difficult without objectives. Objectives help determine which are the major topics, which topics should precede others, how much time should be spent on certain areas, and how the parts of a session are related to each other.

- The selection of teaching methods and materials is facilitated by clear statements of expected learning. If I know that students must be able to apply construction techniques in a workplace setting, I can select strategies that provide the opportunity for experiential learning.

- Feedback and evaluation are clearer when everyone has a shared understanding of the goals. If our objective in an introductory psychology course is to define and give examples of behavior for each of Piaget's developmental stages, then when students can, indeed, define and give examples, the objective is met.

Finally, objectives enhance our communication with administrators, colleagues, and community or professional groups.

- Colleagues who teach other courses in a program can review our objectives and determine what they reasonably can expect students to know when they enter their courses.

- Similarly, colleagues who teach courses that precede or are related to ours can minimize redundancy or overlap between their work and ours.

- Curriculum and evaluation committees can coordinate instruction within and across programs in their institutions or departments.

- Objectives can be shared among teachers who work in similar subject areas or programs but at different institutions or organizations.

- Professional associations or community groups can get a clear picture as to what students are doing in our courses and programs.

Concerns about Objectives

Although objectives are commonly used in curriculum development, often-raised concerns about their use must be considered. These questions may come from learners, instructors, and others in the educational setting.

First, students sometimes feel overwhelmed or intimidated by objectives. This occurs when they are presented with a long list of objectives, when they have no or little input into them, and when the objectives contain discipline-specific language they have not yet learned. Presenting fewer or more general objectives, involving students in their development (if possible), and avoiding or explaining jargon helps to reassure students.

Second, students worry that objectives may restrict their learning, stifle creativity and innovation, or prevent them from following personal interests related to the instruction. Students who are more self-directed may see objectives as inhibiting their autonomy. Learner involvement in the development of objectives is the best way to counteract this concern. It should also be clear that objectives are flexible, negotiable, and act as guideposts rather than fences.

I have often heard learners complain that objectives handed out on the first day of class or at the beginning of a session are never referred to again. In this case, the objectives appear to be meaningless, especially if discussions, readings, or evaluation procedures are not linked to them. We should be careful that the rest of the instructional plan follows from the objectives, and we should stop and review where we are in relation to the objectives on a regular basis. Even in a short, informal learning session, there is a place to ask, Where are we in working toward our objectives? Are there changes we should make? Is everyone confident that they are learning what was set out in the objectives?

Some of the uneasiness expressed by instructors about objectives is similar to that of their students. In these cases, it would be good for instructor and learners to address their concerns together.

Sometimes teachers believe that writing objectives is too time-consuming and detracts from other more productive work. Some misperceptions about the amount of detail necessary may account for this reluctance. If we feel obligated to produce ten or twenty objectives for each class, the task indeed is overwhelming and counterproductive. The number of objectives and degree of detail required does depend on and vary according to the level of instruction and subject area, but if we feel we are wasting too much time preparing objectives, we probably are. The use of objectives per se is not at fault here; it is a matter of overdoing it, being too detailed, writing too many objectives for a simple segment of learning. I still recall, many years later, reviewing curriculum for a nursing assistants' program in which thirty objectives were listed for bed making, objectives to which, naturally enough, neither the teachers nor the students paid much attention.

As do students, instructors sometimes worry that an explicit statement of objectives will lead to a rigid instructional approach. They fear that, somehow, once the objectives are written, learner interests or relevant current issues can no longer be incorporated into their classes. If objectives are regarded this way, as unchanging rules dictating what will happen, rigidity certainly will result. However, there is always room for change—for adding new topics, revising the focus, discarding content in which no one is interested. It is a good idea to regularly review and negotiate objectives over a course or even during a one-or two-day workshop. Do we still want to do this? Does anyone have anything to add? Has our discussion of this topic led us to change what we want to learn?

Another concern of instructors is that objectives may stifle creativity, independent thinking, and critical questioning. If exactly what to learn is known, students can just memorize material without thought or question will not learn to think for themselves. Two issues are involved here. First is the perception that objectives can be written only for basic knowledge or rote learning. Although many textbooks or learning modules primarily present examples of low-level objectives, which are easier to write, objectives certainly can be written for high-level, creative, and critical thinking skills and content. The second part of this perception is based on the assumption that objectives are low level by nature, and therefore educators may see objectives as making learning "too easy." However, good objectives encourage meaningful learning. If our students engage in meaningful learning and are evaluated accordingly, we should be proud of our joint accomplishments.

Other people in the educational community sometimes express the same concerns as those of learners and teachers. However, these administrators, colleagues, or professional and community groups do have some specific questions as well.

Potential employers, from the professions, business, or industry often say that they are not consulted when objectives are developed and that the objectives of a program do not reflect their expectations of the students they hire. When this is an issue, potential employers should be brought in to help develop objectives or asked for feedback on objectives, especially at the program level.

In some venues, objectives are developed by curriculum consultants, administrators, or central office staff and handed down to instructors. In these cases, the individuals who write the objectives often say that teachers and students are not following them carefully. However, if people not doing the teaching or learning develop objectives, good communication between those writing the objectives and those doing the teaching and learning must exist. Second, these curriculum developers must recognize that flexibility is an essential characteristic of good teaching.

How to Write Objectives

Writing good objectives does take time, practice, and feedback. In some subjects and levels where the content is more concrete and the learned behavior more observable, the process is easier. However, regardless of how complex, abstract, factual or subjective the subject is, it is possible to create interesting, challenging, and meaningful objectives. The following guidelines may be helpful and can be used whether writing objectives in advance of a course or session, in collaboration with learners in a course, or as a guide for learners in developing their own objectives.

List the topics or goals of the instruction, using whatever degree of detail seems appropriate. Examples of what might be stated are: learning to construct multiple-choice tests; creating a Web page; becoming familiar with the themes in the novels of Thomas Mann; or relating well to clients.

Try to make the items on the list as clear as possible. Will everyone understand them in the same way? Can a more specific term be used? In traditional instructional design models all objectives must be observable, that is, be stated in terms of a performance or product that can be seen. Sometimes, this is impossible, but it should be possible to detect or infer that the learning has taken place. Or, the students themselves should know clearly whether they have reached the objective even if an outside observer may not see a concrete result. Ask what student responses, characteristics, or behaviors might represent the learning. For example, students studying the themes of Thomas Mann's novels might be able to identify and discuss the theme of one or more novels; relating well to clients could mean that clients make positive statements or that both client and student express satisfaction with the interaction.

For each statement of what is to be learned, consider the degree of detail or specificity necessary. How much to include depends on the subject area, the level of instruction, and the characteristics of the learners. Perhaps some statements should be subdivided for clarity or combined for convenience. For remedial instruction or for lower levels, the steps will be smaller and the objectives more detailed. At higher levels, instruction encompasses broader concepts, syntheses of ideas, and critical thinking and the objectives must reflect this.

Consider, for each objective, the circumstances or conditions under which the learning takes place. Is a certain kind of software necessary? Can students download information from the Web? Does a task need to be done within a certain amount of time? Is there room for error? When necessary, conditions of this nature should be made explicit in the objectives.

Have someone review and comment on objectives if at all possible. Colleagues teaching the same subject, individuals who have completed the course, or an instructional designer or faculty developer can give helpful feedback. Since the goal is to ensure that the objectives are clear to others, good communication is essential. People who agree to comment on the objectives can be asked specific questions both to make their job easier and to elicit the information we want. Colleagues can be asked whether the objectives reflect the content of the course; former students can indicate whether the objectives identify the things they learned from the course; and an instructional designer or faculty developer can review for clarity, format, and freedom from jargon.

Finally, discuss the objectives with students and, if necessary, revise them according to their comments. Ideally, adult students should be involved in the development of their own learning objectives. When this is not possible due to institutional or time constraints or the demands of certification boards, at least examine the objectives together with the students. Even if the instructional content is mandated by someone else, objectives can be revised in order to make them easier to understand and work with. Under most circumstances, though, teachers of specific courses or sessions develop their own objectives and can ask students for feedback. Are the objectives clear? Do they represent their interests and needs? Should additions or deletions be made? This collaborative process not only improves the objectives, but also fosters student involvement and motivation. Students who feel some ownership of the learning objectives care more about achieving them.

Types of Objectives I may be very adept at understanding theoretical models but unable to learn a second language easily. Another person may quickly master the intricacies of a car engine but struggle to memorize facts and figures. We know that there are different kinds of learning, and it is also fairly clear that they are best facilitated by different teaching strategies. Anyone who has labored to learn a mechanical task by reading a manual, then learned it quickly when someone demonstrated how to do it, realizes this basic principle of teaching and learning. A fundamental part of writing objectives is determining what kind of learning is involved. We can then base our selection of methods, materials, and evaluation techniques on the nature and level of the learning.

Domains of Learning

In the 1970s and 1980s, classification systems of learning were derived from cognitive psychology (see Gagné, 1975, for example). However, it was in 1956 that the most widely used description of kinds of learning was developed by Benjamin Bloom and a committee of his colleagues (Bloom, 1956; Krathwohl, Bloom, and Masia, 1964). Shortly thereafter, Simpson (1966) defined the psychomotor domain in more detail. More than half a century later, it is Bloom's taxonomy that comes up consistently in any search for domains of learning, and it is Bloom's taxonomy that is still at the heart of nearly all traditional or conventional instructional design and program planning. Bloom defined three domains of learning: cognitive, affective, and psychomotor, which are described in detail in the next sections.

Some theorists have elaborated on the basic taxonomy; Hauenstein (1998), for example, proposed an additional domain that is a composite of the original domains. Pohl (2000) slightly revised the wording and the order of the levels of learning in the cognitive domain. MacKeracher (2004) discusses, in addition to the cognitive processes, the emotional, social, physical, and spiritual aspects of learning. Effective learning is not only analytical, but also can be holistic, she suggests, and therefore non-verbal, non-logical, and non-rational.

- The *cognitive domain* includes all intellectual processes: the recall of definitions, terms, names, and dates; the comprehension of concepts; the application of principles or formulae to the solution of problems; the analysis of ideas presented by others; the integration and synthesis of ideas and concepts; and critical evaluation or judgment of theories, assumptions, and ideas.

- The *affective domain* encompasses values, attitudes, beliefs, emotions, motivation, and interests. In most situations, there is, at least, the implicit objective that participants will be interested in the subject or that they will be motivated to learn. In other areas, such as the professions of nursing or social work or medicine, the values and attitudes of learners are an integral part of learning. The recent emphasis on emotional learning and relational learning (Dirkx, 2008) would fall into this domain.

- The *psychomotor domain* incorporates all physical performance. In physical education where students are learning how to play tennis or increasing their general fitness level, it is clear that the focus is on the psychomotor domain. It is also a substantial element in areas such as crafts, dance, second language learning (the physical production of sounds), medicine, and nursing. The psychomotor domain includes the finely coordinated movements that are a part of technical skills (filling a tooth, using a lathe, drawing), as well as non-verbal communication or portraying feelings through body movements (drama, interpersonal skills in psychiatry or social work). Recently, adult educators are paying attention to embodied learning (Freiler, 2008), which is described as learning "through the body." It bears some resemblance to psychomotor learning, but is not as broad a concept.

In many settings the cognitive, affective, and psychomotor domains are intertwined. In the affective and psychomotor areas, there is almost always a cognitive component as well. In learning a technical skill, one must first "know" the steps to be performed in a cognitive sense, and then practice the physical skill. Affective objectives involving the development of value systems also include the cognitive knowledge on which those values are based.

Levels of Learning

Within each of the cognitive, affective, and psychomotor domains, learning varies in level or complexity. Students learning to identify varieties of trees are engaged in a quite different process from those who are developing a woodlot management plan. Participants in a medical ethics workshop who are reading about perspectives on assisted suicide are working at a level different from those who are formulating a policy on the issue for their hospital.

For each domain and level of learning, I give three examples of objectives. Although, traditionally, objectives are usually expressed in the following form, "The learner will be able to...," I advocate a less formal wording. When students participate in the development of objectives, they may prefer to state, "We will..." or "We plan to learn to..." In more individualized settings, learners may wish to express their objectives in the first person: "I will..." At other times, it may be most appropriate to use the phrasing, "You will...," and there may also be occasions where "Students will..." is still the most comfortable choice. I illustrate various formats here.

Cognitive Domain   Bloom (1956) developed a six-level taxonomy for the cognitive domain. The taxonomy is hierarchical in that learning at the lower, simpler levels precedes learning at the higher, more complex levels. Krathwohl (1998) renames each of these levels, using simpler verb forms, and reorders two of the levels. Hauenstein (1998) renames one level and elaborates on the content of others.

The lowest level (the simplest type of learning) in the cognitive domain is called *knowledge* by Bloom. This label may be troublesome to some as the word "knowledge" usually includes a much broader spectrum of intellectual activity. Krathwohl (1998) renames this level *remember.* Hauenstein (1998) calls it *conceptualization* and identifies within it three subcategories—identification, definition, and generalization. This first level of cognitive learning includes the recognition and recall of basic facts.

> We will label from memory the parts of the ear on a drawing of the ear.

> After reading this text, you should be able to define each of the three domains of learning in an instructional design model.

> I plan to recognize at least ten varieties of flowers from sketches.

The knowledge level does not necessarily include an understanding of the material. It comprises basic rote learning.

Bloom's second level of learning is *comprehension*, renamed *understand*, by Krathwohl. The learner demonstrates understanding or comprehension by putting things in his or her own words or giving illustrations and examples of a concept.

> I will illustrate each of the three domains of learning with examples from my own subject area.

> You should be able to describe the behaviors associated with autism in your own words.

> We will be able to explain the procedure for performing a binary search for a name in a telephone directory.

It is sometimes difficult to be sure that objectives at this level actually do involve comprehension and not merely rote knowledge. If students can use a unique wording, expand on a definition or concept, or illustrate something, we can be fairly sure that their responses do not merely involve memorization of material.

The third level in the cognitive domain is referred to as *application* (Bloom, 1956), or simply, apply, according to Krathwohl's (1998) proposed revision. Rules, principles, and basic knowledge are used to solve problems or are applied to a new context. Thus, this level involves the application of previously learned knowledge in another unfamiliar situation.

> After this session, students should be able to use the t-test formula to determine whether or not the means of two sets of data are significantly different from each other.

> I plan to write objectives in the affective domain of learning for my course.

> I want to be able to use Google to find information on Japanese beetles.

At the application level of learning, there is usually a clear and correct product.

Analysis is the fourth level in the hierarchy. Krathwohl (1998) uses the verb form and calls this level *analyze*. The components of a theory, model, concept, or idea are taken apart, and the relationships between them are examined. Comparisons are made, similarities and differences identified, and the distinction between major and minor topics is clarified.

> We will identify and describe the five components of a short story, as well as noting any elements that are missing, in a story we have not read before.

> You will be able to explain at least three major differences between the theories of Freud and Jung.

> Students should be able to compare and contrast two philosophies of adult education.

Analysis is dependent on the understanding of the components of the topics under scrutiny. In some cases, application may not be a prerequisite for analysis.

The next level in Bloom's taxonomy is *synthesis*. Krathwohl calls this *create* and places it at the highest level of learning. Synthesis encompasses an array of complex processes — the putting together of information, concepts, or positions from several sources into one product. Writing an essay, designing a web site, or formulating a proposal requires the synthesis of ideas.

> I will write a research proposal, including a research question, a brief review of the literature, and a suggested methodology for answering the question.

> The learner will create a web site for marketing a new product of his or her choice.

> After you have read this book, you should be able to prepare a course outline that includes objectives, the sequence of instruction, teaching methods and materials, and strategies for evaluating both learning and teaching.

The synthesis level of learning is where we bring together the parts and demonstrate a full, holistic understanding of what has been studied.

The *evaluation* level in the cognitive domain involves making judgments of quality based on criteria. Critical thinking, a goal of most adult education, requires that students reach this level of learning. It is an objective evaluation based on a cognitive knowledge of what constitutes a good product. Krathwohl (1998) calls this simply *evaluate*, but he reverses the order in the hierarchy, suggesting it comes before create (or synthesis).

> After reading a research article, I will write a critique describing both the strengths of the research and any methodological flaws in the procedure used.

> You will evaluate the strengths and limitations of this instructional design book, including as a basis of comparison, the evaluation of one other textbook with a similar purpose.

> Students will critically analyze the language of a text in relation to power relations based on race, class, gender, and sexual orientation.

The evaluation level is a goal in more advanced instruction. A good knowledge of the subject area is needed before learners can make valid critical judgments.

Affective Domain In the affective domain, the hierarchical aspect of learning is less clear. Also, it becomes much more difficult to prepare objectives that are observable and concrete when dealing with the values, beliefs, interests, and emotional responses of individuals. Traditional instructional designers argue that students should exhibit some behavior that is indicative of a change in attitude or values. In transformative learning theory (Mezirow, 2003), which describes changes in values, beliefs, and assumptions, action on the learning is a part of the theoretical model, but it is not consistently the case that a person is able to act on a changed value or belief.

Say we hope that students will enjoy reading poetry or develop their own code of professional values in nursing. There may very well be behaviors that indicate these goals have been reached. For example, students may read poetry in their spare time or talk to their peers about their professional values. But they also may demonstrate enjoyment in ways that we cannot observe or validate. Or students may do things other than the ones we have identified to indicate this kind of learning has taken place.

If there is an objective that students will read at least two books of poetry at home as an indicator of enjoyment, will students do this only because it is an expectation, not because they enjoy poetry? It seems that simple learner self-report can be used, with the assumption being that people will be honest about their learning.

Learning that is communicative in nature (to do with understanding ourselves, others, and social norms) is validated by people agreeing on what is true in a certain context or culture. Most people would agree on what "enjoy" means. Most people would probably also recognize enjoyment in progress.

Krathwohl, Bloom, and Masia (1964) describe five levels of learning in the affective domain. Hauenstein (1998) redefines the highest two levels, but otherwise follows the original taxonomy.

At the receiving level, the learner simply attends to and becomes aware of a value, belief, or attitude. He or she may listen to someone express an attitude on an issue, attend an art exhibit, or listen to a selection of music. No change takes place, but the student willingly receives and considers the attitude or belief.

> I will go on a walking tour of the old section of Montreal in order to observe architectural styles.
>
> We will listen to Tchaikovsky's Piano Concerto No. 1.
>
> The group will read two poems by Sylvia Plath.

At this lowest level, there need not be any response. The students are exposed to something that may, as learning goes on, change their values or beliefs.

At the *responding* level of the affective domain, students actively attend to others' values, opinions, or beliefs. They respond in either a positive or negative manner — they express an opinion on the issue.

> Students will enjoy and express enjoyment of tennis during their lessons.
>
> While reading this book, you will become interested in how instructional design can be used in adult education and talk about it with your colleagues.
>
> We will take an active part in discussions on how institutions can help make LGBTQ students feel safe and welcomed.

The responding level of the affective domain is demonstrated by the expression of interest, enjoyment, opinion, or attitudes. There is not necessarily a commitment to the response.

Valuing is the third level of the affective domain. Students begin to show consistency in and commitment to beliefs, values, and attitudes. A value is preferred and acted upon, although the relationship among values is not yet established.

> We will not go back to smoking cigarettes after we finish our smoking cessation program.

> Because of my course in women's studies, I will actively protest against the use of sexist language in my other courses.

> At the end of this safety training program, we will be much more conscientious about following the rules and regulations in the workplace.

When our teaching includes affective objectives, we usually hope that students will at least reach this valuing level. We want people to act on their changed values or beliefs.

At the fourth level, *organization*, learners organize values, beliefs, and attitudes into a system, determine the interrelationships among them, and develop priorities. Rather than demonstrating commitment to isolated values, students display a more complex value system. Hauenstein (1998) suggests that this level be called believing. Believing involves trusting and making a commitment to a value as a guiding principle. He suggests that sets of values are organized into beliefs, so although some of the details of his taxonomy are at odds with the original system used by Krathwohl et al. (1964), the basic concept is similar.

> We will study several views of the ethics of social worker and patient interactions and formulate a personal set of guidelines.

> I will make a list of the things I value about teaching, put those items in order of importance to me, and write a short statement as to my philosophy of practice.

> You will write an article for the local newspaper on the issue of conservation of resources versus technological advancement.

The organization level of the affective domain is distinguished from the lower levels by the existence of several values, beliefs, or attitudes, and the exploration of the relationships among them.

The fifth and highest level in the affective domain is *characterization by a value*, according to Krathwohl et al. (1964). Students have assimilated a belief or value system to such an extent that they are characterized by that value—"She is a feminist"; "He is a scholar of German history." The values become integral to a person's world-view or philosophy. Hauenstein (1998) calls this level *behaving*, defining it as a "disposition to demonstrate and modify a behavior in accord with a value or belief" (p.77). It reflects a habit of mind.

> I will dedicate my life to the study of music.
>
> Students in this program will become caring professional educators.
>
> I will leave my current position and become an entrepreneur.

It is not that often that we develop objectives at this level for others, except as program goals. When a person already has a great interest in and commitment to a field, she may set such goals for herself.

Psychomotor Domain The newer work on embodied learning calls for "holistic, integrative learning approaches wherein the body is made more visible as a source of knowledge and a site for learning" (Freiler, 2008, p. 44). It emphasizes the role of the body in learning and helps us move away from a strictly cognitive focus in teaching and learning, but it does not yet help us to organize or design instruction beyond urging that embodiment be included in a variety of learning contexts. I return to the traditional taxonomies for this discussion.

In the psychomotor domain, various organizational schemes have been developed, some hierarchical and others categorical. Simpson's (1966) taxonomy is hierarchical in nature and so it aligns with the cognitive and affective taxonomies used here. The objectives at the lower levels are simpler and generally need to be learned before the higher levels.

Hauenstein (1998) is critical of Simpson's and others' work in that the taxonomies have tended to emphasize the "motor" rather than the "psycho" components of psychomotor learning. He reminds us that taxonomies in general should be useful and relevant in the teaching and learning process and should be inclusive of all abilities and skills, and they should be arranged following a consistent principle of order, such as from simple to complex learning. Hauenstein synthesizes categories from several taxonomies and creates some new labels in order to present a clear and comprehensive system for working with psycho-motor learning. I will use Hauenstein's terminology, but also refer to the more familiar taxonomy prepared by Simpson (1966).

Both Hauenstein and Simpson call the first level of psychomotor learning *perception*. This level includes the awareness of objects in the environment arrived at through the senses and the association of those objects with the task to be performed. It is seen to be the basis for all psychomotor learning in much the same way that receiving is the basis for affective learning.

> We will learn to discriminate among the colors to be used in oil painting.
>
> I will learn to recognize the angle at which a squash ball bounces from the wall before I swing my racquet.
>
> Students will be able to distinguish, by touch, four different types of fabric.

If students do not possess the basic perceptual skills that precede mastery of a psychomotor skill, it is difficult to go any further. Anyone who has spent a few hours hopelessly swinging a racquet through the air while the ball sails by knows that perception is the foundation of psychomotor performance.

According to Hauenstein, the second level of psychomotor learning is *simulation*. This is similar to Simpson's third level of *guided response*. (Hauenstein has no category equivalent to Simpson's second level, called *set*, being mentally or physically prepared for the action.) At the simulation level, the student tries out or duplicates a pattern of specific actions. Actions are imitated and coordination is learned. Sometimes actions are performed by trial and error, then adjustments are made based on feedback from the performance itself. That is, we try to do something, it does not quite work, we try it again in a slightly different way; it is better and we repeat this process until the actions are correct and smooth.

> I will imitate the instructor by following her as she executes one parallel turn on downhill skis.
>
> We will practice making one edge of a board smooth and straight using a jack plane.

> By following the guidelines and photographs in the text, we
> will cook a white wine sauce of the proper consistency.

The simulation level is the first physical step in psychomotor performance. By following guidelines, modeling themselves after an expert, or trial and error practice, students acquire the skills necessary to go on.

Hauenstein's third level is called *conformation*. Skills are sufficiently practiced so as to conform to a standard or criteria. This level is also similar to Simpson's guided response. Repeated practice, accompanied by feedback, leads to a performance having the necessary qualities and characteristics of the skill.

> I will learn to receive a football hike from the center, back
> step, read the field, and pass on target.

> We will practice plucking guitar strings in the correct
> sequence.

> You should be able create charts and graphs using Word.

At the conformation level, aptitudes and actions are integrated into a complex pattern or task. It meets certain criteria and is recognized as being competently executed.

At Hauenstein's fourth level, *production*, the behaviors learned through imitation and practice become habitual or routine. In addition, the skills are used routinely to produce a desired act or procedure. Simpson's *complex overt response* is comparable. Students become efficient and natural in their performance. Most of us use the keyboard or drive a car in this way. Our body performs automatically.

> I will become efficient at using the herringbone step to go
> uphill on cross-country skis.

> Students will smoothly administer an intravenous needle.

> Students will automatically set the shutter speed, aperture,
> and determine depth of field on a digital camera.

In psychomotor learning, it is almost always our goal to reach this independent and routine level of performance. We should not have to think about what we are doing; we do it naturally.

The fifth and highest level in Hauenstein's taxonomy is called *mastery*. Students "seek to become better, to do better, to excel, to be able to demonstrate their expertise and artistry" (p. 96). Mastery is the ability both to originate and perfect skills. As such, it encompasses two of Simpson's levels of learning, *adaptation and origination.*

> I will learn to landscape and maintain the grounds of a commercial building regardless of the weather.
>
> Students will learn to conduct a preliminary check-up on patients at accident sites.
>
> We will develop a set of secret hand signals to communicate among team members in a soccer match.

Students learn to choose the movements or skills to be used based on the immediately preceding action. A well-developed repertoire of skills and the knowledge of when each is appropriate are required. Students have also completely mastered the component parts of a skill and are now able to create new ways of combining them. In some subject areas, students can also originate a completely new way of performing.

Objectives and the Adult Learner

In Chapter Two, I outlined some characteristics of the adult learner that we should consider in our use of objectives. In brief, adults prefer to be self-directed in many situations. They like to have something to say about what they learn. They choose programs, courses, or workshops based on their interests and needs. There is diversity in any group of adults in terms of their experiences, values, gender, and culture. How can we incorporate these and other important concepts from the adult learning literature into our use of objectives?

Sometimes objectives need to be prepared in advance of a course, workshop, or seminar. Some institutions require this, usually with the good intention of protecting and informing students. Other people—professional associations, government agencies, industry, and department heads—sometimes control curriculum decisions.

And sometimes, we just do not have any choice: if, for example, we are giving a workshop in another part of the country, we need to prepare before we ever see a student.

When this is the case, when we prepare objectives in advance of the sessions, we must try to find out as much about the learners as possible. There are different ways of doing this, depending on the context and situation.

> Sometimes a needs assessment can be conducted, either formally or informally, though informally is usually best. For example, prior to an in-service workshop, a short questionnaire can be included with the registration forms to ask participants about their previous experience and special interests.

> Program directors or coordinators are often pleased to collect information about what students want to learn by holding an orientation meeting, talking with potential students, or sending out letters or e-mail communications to elicit responses.

> For courses being offered in structured programs, information about the learners is often available from records or from other instructors in the same program.

> In a general interest course or a continuing education course, we can use the first session to discuss participants' interests, background, needs, and experiences.

> That participants have chosen to attend a session gives us some basic information. A session on the use of insecticides in grape growing will be attended by people who are growing grapes or planning to grow grapes and who need this information for their work.

Whenever possible, students should have an opportunity to discuss and have input into objectives. The more involvement people have with the planning of the learning experience, the more it will be theirs; they will feel ownership and responsibility, and interest and motivation will be stimulated.

> Regardless of the length of the instruction, whether it is a one-year course or a two-hour training session, learners can have something to say about the objectives. In a course, the

first class or a part of the first class can be devoted to such a discussion. In a two-hour workshop, the first 10 or 15 minutes can be spent talking about the learning goals.

When learners are unfamiliar with the subject or when the content is mostly predetermined, lengthy debate over the objectives is frustrating. In this situation, it is usually best to hand out the prepared objectives and ask participants to read them over and make suggestions for changes, additions, or deletions. The number of changes, in these circumstances, will be few. Most people, in a new situation, are reluctant to make major changes to prepared materials. Asking them to do so will only increase their discomfort or anxiety.

With a more independent, mature, experienced, or confident group, input into the objectives should be requested before handing out a prepared list. The session can begin with a general discussion of the parameters of the course, workshop, or meeting, then move into what people expect to get out of the session. Surprisingly often expectations match prepared objectives fairly well. If not, we modify our plans on the spot.

In a course or series of workshops that extends over several sessions, objectives can be reviewed and discussed with students regularly, perhaps even as often as in each session. As students gain experience and expertise with the subject and confidence and trust within the group, they will be more able and willing to make suggestions for changes. Even if the objectives are not revised, periodic review reminds everyone of the structure and goals of the course.

When we work with students who have a good background in the subject, we can develop objectives collaboratively. This is not practical in a one-time workshop or any session that is shorter than one day but is extremely worthwhile otherwise.

Participants can work in small groups to generate topics of interest. A brainstorming technique, in which all possible topics are listed, then prioritized and categorized, often works well.

The small group lists can then be presented to the larger group to be discussed and questioned. Overlapping topics can be eliminated at this stage and further categorizing can be done (grouping of similar or related topics).

The instructor should add topics he or she feels are critical to the course and, if appropriate, point out topics that fall outside of the sphere of the course.

The list of topics can then be ranked or rated by participants, or, if the group is relatively small, people can come to consensus on the final list through discussion.

Topics can be translated into objectives by the students or by the instructor. The final list of objectives can be reviewed for omissions. It is a good idea to check with students to see if they feel their interests and needs are fully represented.

With an experienced, independent group who has diverse interests and needs, we can negotiate objectives individually with each learner. The educator become a resource person and facilitator in this process. With larger groups, this is hard to do.

We need to think of our learners as active participants in the design of instruction. The amount of responsibility they take depends to some extent on their maturity, experience, and self-directedness, though students with less experience or background can surprise us with their interest and involvement in planning for learning when we give them a chance to participate.

Summary

Objectives help students and instructors understand where they are headed in the teaching and learning process. They need not be restrictive or constraining; they need not prevent us from following exciting tangents or changing directions. They are merely statements we use to clarify for others and ourselves what we think we are doing in our classrooms, workshops, seminars, and training programs. As such, they provide the basis for organizing topics into a sequence, deciding on teaching methods, finding materials and resources, and evaluating what has been learned. Sometimes we may end up reaching an unforeseen goal, and sometimes this indeed may be a better goal in retrospect, but at least we had a place to set out to reach when we started.

Writing good objectives is no different from writing anything else clearly. Starting with a list of interests, topics, or aspects of a subject to be included in the instruction, we can then determine what we plan to learn about these topics and put our aspirations in simple, straightforward language. Since, as instructors, we are subject area specialists or experts, we may tend not to notice the terminology or jargon that is so familiar to us. Having others review and comment on our objectives helps avoid this pitfall. Student involvement in reviewing and, ideally, preparing objectives adds to their value.

Although there are different ways to classify types of learning, I use the classic distinction between cognitive, affective, and psycho-motor learning as a basis for objective writing. Within each of these domains are levels of learning, ranging from simple to complex. The use of a hierarchical taxonomy is especially helpful in sequencing instruction and evaluating learning.

There are several strategies for making objectives more meaningful to adult learners. Obtaining information about students' backgrounds, needs, and interests and incorporating this into the objectives will increase comfort and interest. To varying degrees, learners can participate in the review, discussion, and preparation of objectives. The more people know about the subject and the more experience they have in working with the concepts involved, the greater can be their involvement in planning the learning experience.

Chapter 4
Sequencing Learning Experiences

The sequence of learning experiences is critical not only for how well we learn, but also for how we feel about learning. Anyone who has struggled to learn from a technical manual without understanding the prerequisite technical language or possessing fundamental knowledge can attest to how difficult and frustrating a learning experience that is. With most cognitive and psychomotor learning, we must master the basics before proceeding to more complex problems or tasks. We cannot, for example, understand the statistical concept of regression without knowing what correlations are, or play a game of racquet ball without having developed the eye-hand coordination necessary to hit the ball. In the affective domain, the importance of sequence is less obvious, but exposure to and understanding of ideas and experiences must occur before we form values. Educators need to consider the sequence of instruction within the context of their practice. Conventional planning models were grounded within a technical rational tradition, but we now recognize that learning takes place through human interactions, is framed by power relations, involves emotions, and exists in a cultural context (Cervero and Wilson, 2006).

In this chapter, I present three sets of strategies for sequencing learning. First, I discuss how *choosing a sequencing strategy* depends on the nature and structure of the knowledge we are working with, the experience and characteristics of the students, the methods and materials we plan to use (which are, in turn, at least partially conditional on the domain and level of learning), and the context of the teaching and learning experience. Second, I present *hierarchical task analysis*, which is commonly used with technical cognitive learning or learning at the lower end of the cognitive taxonomy. Third, I consider *conceptual sequencing strategies* for learning at the higher levels of the cognitive and affective domains. This includes communicative learning where the knowledge is socially constructed and emancipatory learning that focuses on personal growth and development. Fourth, I describe *procedural analysis*, a method of examining the components of psychomotor learning tasks.

Choosing a Sequencing Strategy

Experienced teachers seem to know intuitively how to create a course outline, arranging topics in an order that works for everyone. However, this expertise is the result of their years of practice, consideration of feedback from their students, and reflection on their work. I still hesitate over the sequence of topics in a course. For example, in an adult education course, I arranged all the topics related to groups — group dynamics, group processes, group work, and difficult groups — one after the other. But by the middle of this section of the course, the students, who were initially very interested in discussing the use of groups in education, were tired of talking about groups and working in groups. They were looking for variety, something I had overlooked in thinking only about the concepts in the content of the course. In another course or situation, with another group of people, however, this sequence might have worked well. When the content itself does not have an inherent structure, educators need to be flexible and ready to revise sequencing strategies when they are not effective.

The first consideration in choosing a sequencing strategy is the nature and structure of the knowledge with which we are working. If the knowledge is technical and in the cognitive domain, *hierarchical task analysis* may be the most useful tool. Technical knowledge is that knowledge which is objective and consists of facts, rules, and principles. It is scientific in nature, that is, it is derived from scientific methods. Understanding how an airplane works, using statistics, doing mathematics, and analyzing the physiology of the human body are all examples of technical knowledge in the cognitive domain. With technical knowledge, the content has an inherent structure. As a result, people usually need to learn certain components before they can grasp others.

If the knowledge is communicative or emancipatory in nature and at the higher levels of the cognitive domain or in the affective domain, what I call *conceptual sequencing strategies* are more likely to be appropriate. Communicative knowledge is subjective, based on understanding others and the social norms of the group, community, or culture within which we live. It is socially constructed; that is, it is considered valid and true because informed people in a group or culture agree that it is true. Emancipatory knowledge is also subjective, focusing on our becoming free from personal and social constraints. Establishing good interpersonal relations with clients or patients, understanding how groups function, increasing personal self-awareness, being aware of how other cultures are different from our own, developing an appreciation for cultural diversity, and challenging hegemony are examples of emancipatory learning on the individual level and the social or political level.

When the knowledge we are working with is in the psychomotor domain or is embodied knowing, *procedural analysis* provides a good basis for sequencing learning. Here, the emphasis is on performing a skill or a set of skills that is primarily physical in nature. As discussed in Chapter Three, cognitive and affective knowledge is intertwined with embodied knowing, but when emphasis is on the physical aspect of the performance, this analysis is the best basis on which to order the learning experience.

If the knowledge is some combination of these three categories, *a mixture of sequencing strategies* probably can be used. Hierarchical task analysis should come first to ensure that the basic prerequisite knowledge is acquired. Conceptual sequencing strategies can be used to organize the overall structure of the course or sessions. Procedural analysis should be applied to the psychomotor components of the learning.

The second consideration in choosing a sequencing strategy comprises the experience and characteristics of the learners. The examples that follow illustrate how these factors are relevant.

When students have little or no background or experience with the content or subject, and the knowledge is technical in nature, a detailed hierarchical task analysis is very useful. Similarly, when students have no experience and the intended learning falls into the psychomotor domain, a procedural analysis is invaluable. As teachers, we are usually experienced subject experts and may not pinpoint the prerequisite learning or be aware of all the components of the performance that have become second nature to us.

When students are experienced in the subject and have already acquired the basic content, conceptual sequencing may be the most appropriate approach, regardless of the kind of knowledge. This way, learning can be made more interesting by being organized around issues, interests, or projects.

When students have clear interests or practical needs in some aspects of a course, workshop, or seminar, their needs and interests should be considered in the sequencing. Getting people immediately involved in learning by placing the most interesting and relevant topic first can build up a momentum of motivation that carries through other necessary but less attractive topics.

Students' learning styles or personality preferences are sometimes important in sequencing instruction. If a creative and enthusiastic group of fashion designers or computer animators must spend the first five classes studying types of fabrics or the technical aspects of using a software package, their frustration may impede their learning. In such a situation, we should be sure to include more divergent, intuitive activities early on in the course before all of the technical prerequisites have been introduced for study.

The third consideration in deciding how to sequence learning includes the methods and materials that will be used. The order of chapters in this book implies that selecting methods and materials follows sequencing, but these aspects of designing instruction may be done together. The following examples show how the choice of methods and materials can influence the sequence of learning.

The use of a variety of methods is important both for maintaining student interest and for connecting with the different learning and personality preferences of students. If methods are matched directly to objectives and objectives are sequenced according to hierarchical task analysis, the same method may be used several times in a row. It may be more important to break up such a sequence by changing methods regardless of the results of the task analysis.

Some methods require more student involvement than others. For these methods to work, it is more important that students are comfortable and trust each other and the teacher. If students are new to a learning situation, anxious, intimidated, or otherwise unsure of themselves, it is often wiser not to expect an immediate high level of involvement or trust. In such a situation, animated discussion or enthusiastic participation in a role-play on the first day is unlikely. A gradual transition from more teacher-centered to more learner-centered methods may be important in planning the sequence.

Certain methods or materials may be available only at specific times. Having a field trip, showing a film, or inviting a guest speaker often depends on outside factors or someone else's schedule.

Some materials, including textbooks, software packages, and instructional modules, have a built-in sequence. Although working with these materials out of sequence is possible (e.g., read chapter five, then chapter one), care must be taken to ensure that other problems are not created, such as gaps in information or confusion caused by cross-referencing.

The fourth consideration in sequencing learning is the context of the teaching and learning experience. Some examples are listed below; others will come to mind in relation to specific contexts.

The time of day of a course or session can have a bearing on its sequencing. If participants have been working all day and are attending a seminar in the evening, or if a class immediately follows the lunch or supper hour, it may be important to start with lively, interesting activities even if your task analysis suggests it is time to learn basic facts.

Group size matters. In a small group, it is easy to find out whether students are able to jump ahead to more complex topics or need more time on some basics. In a large group, not only are the students more likely to vary in background, ability, and interests, but also it is harder to find out where everyone is. Sequencing, in this case, needs to be more carefully based on an analysis of the content.

Workshops or seminars held in a work setting may be influenced by characteristics of the setting. Often the demands of the institution or organization take precedence over teaching or at least compete with it. Patients' needs in a hospital, for example, come before learners' needs. Or, the work being conducted in a factory on a particular day may not match what the students should be learning on that day. The ideal sequence of learning cannot always be carried out.

Facilities, such as computer labs, dark rooms, kilns, or studios, may not always be available at exactly the right time for the learning experience or may not be spacious enough to accommodate all the students in a group. The sequence of topics may need to be adjusted to fit availability rather than the desired order of learning.

Hierarchical Task Analysis

A hierarchical task analysis is based on the assumption that the structure of the knowledge to be learned is hierarchical in nature. It is a procedure by which we can determine the specific aspects of learning that must precede others to best facilitate mastery of an objective or goal. Task analysis techniques were developed in the late 1960s and popularized by Gagné (1975). Today, task analysis procedures are still very much the same as they were in the 1960s and 1970s (for example, see Randall, Klein, and Hoffman, 2006; Shepherd, 2001). Hierarchical task analysis is most appropriately used to examine technical knowledge in the cognitive domain.

Although conducting a hierarchical task analysis takes time and a thorough knowledge of the concepts being analyzed, it is clearly a worthwhile endeavor. First of all, in some subjects, learners literally cannot achieve an objective without certain prerequisite knowledge. As teachers, we are often so familiar with the content in question that we are no longer aware of its prerequisites and cannot understand why students have trouble. Second, it can be very valuable for students to have and work with a copy of a task analysis. This outline can be used as a self-assessment checklist and study guide. Third, a comprehensive analysis of course content reveals the levels of learning included in that course. Sometimes, it is a surprise to discover that the majority of the objectives are at the knowledge or comprehension level of learning when, in fact, our intent was to reach higher levels of learning. Finally, task analysis can help with the evaluation of learning. If the subject is organized in a hierarchical structure, then achieving higher level objectives indicates that the prerequisites have also been learned.

I describe the procedure for doing a task analysis, then give an example of how this can be carried out.

Procedure

Step 1: Select the objective or objectives for analysis, keeping in mind that this procedure is most appropriate for technical knowledge in the cognitive domain. The final or overall objective of a course or segment of a course may be chosen or, alternatively, only the more difficult and complex objectives within a course. A hierarchical task analysis is most useful for those objectives with which students tend to have the most trouble or those that seem to be the hardest to teach for any reason.

Step 2: Considering one objective at a time, ask, "What must the person know in order to achieve this objective?" List these components. Order does not matter at this point.

Step 3: For each of the items listed in step 2, again ask, "What must the person know in order to learn this?" Continue to list the components of learning.

Step 4: Repeat this process until the answers to the question are things that students are likely to know. When it is not clear what students might already know, it is better to continue on to a slightly simpler level rather than to start the sequencing at a too-complex level. This can always be revised later.

Step 5: Go back to the lists from steps 3 and 4 and arrange each item in a diagram such as is shown in Figure 4-1. The simplest learning is at the bottom, and each arrow indicates that what is in the lower box has to be learned before exposure to what is in the upper box. Where two boxes lead into one, both of these things have to be learned before the next learning can take place.

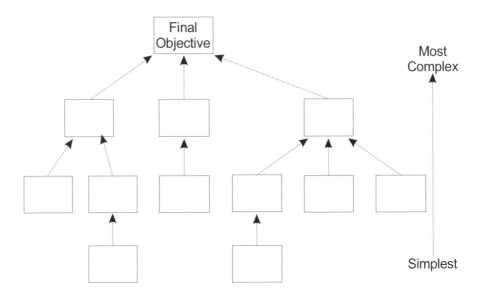

Fig. 4-1.

Step 6: Ask an experienced learner or a colleague who is a subject expert to review the analysis. Explain the diagram and ask the reviewer to look for gaps and relationships between items that do not seem right.

Step 7: Try out the analysis with students. If there are places where individuals experience difficulty or confusion, this indicates that something is missing or out of order. If students are able to meet a higher level objective without the content of the preceding one, this also indicates a flaw in logic.

Example:

The following example describes a task analysis of one objective for a course called "Introduction to Data Structures." The educator, Mark, was relatively inexperienced in terms of teaching, but knew the content extremely well.

Step 1: Mark and I chose to analyze one objective that he found especially hard to teach. It was defined as follows: *"The student will write a set of modular subroutines to operate on an object."*

Step 2: I asked Mark, "What do students have to know before they can start to learn this?" He produced the following list: Students must be able to:

 (a) determine what operations are necessary;

 (b) describe the use to which the object will be put;

 (c) justify a choice for the implementation of the object;

 (d) choose a suitable programming language;

 (e) be able to write programs in a suitable language.

Step 3: Mark and I then took each of these five components and asked the question again. If, for example, students are going to (a) determine what operations are necessary, then what do they have to know before they can start to learn this? Mark added some further components. He knew that before students could begin to carry out item (a) they would need to:

 (a1) describe the use to which the object will be put.

Here, Mark expected students would have the knowledge necessary to describe the use to which the object will be put when they entered the course. Thus, component (b) *describe the use to which the object will be put* was labeled *entry behavior.*

Mark identified five things students must do before being able to carry out component (c) *justify the choice for the implementation of an object.* These were:

 (c1) determine for a variety of implementations the "cost" of the operations;

 (c2) analyze an operation for a given implementation;

(c3) describe all possible implementations of the object;

(c4) compare two different implementations;

(c5) determine the criteria for evaluation of an implementation.

Before students could learn to meet objective (d) *choose a suitable programming language,* Mark decided they would have to be able to do two things:

(d1) describe available languages and the features of those languages;

(d2) describe the efficiency of the available languages.

As for component (e) *write programs in a suitable language,* all students in Mark's course were expected to be competent programmers. We listed this as entry behavior.

Step 4: Mark and I went back and examined the skills or knowledge listed in Step 3 and asked ourselves the same question, "What do students need to know before they can start to learn this?" The first was:

(a1) describe the use to which the object will be put.

Mark was certain that students would know this already. We labeled it as *entry behavior.*

We had already determined that item (b) on the previous list was something students would know coming into the course, so we were able to skip that item.

Next was:

(c1) determine for a variety of implementations the "cost" of the operations.

Mark thought that the next two items, (c2) and (c3), were actually prerequisites for this objective. We therefore labeled (c2) and (c3) as *prerequisite learning* for (c1).

Asking what students would need to know before they could (c2) *analyze an operation for a given implementation* yielded one further item:

(c2.1) the student should be able to perform a worst case analysis of an operation on an implementation.

For (c3) *compare all possible implementations of the object*, Mark indicated that students would be able to do this. We added the label: *entry behavior*.

For (c4) *compare two different implementations*, Mark decided that this item might be included already in the previous statement. If students can compare implementations, he said, they can compare two or more, it does not matter. We therefore labeled this as *may be redundant*.

For (c5) *determine the criteria for evaluation of an implementation*, Mark thought that this item, too, might be already included in the comparison of implementations. We temporarily labeled this as *may be redundant*.

Our further analyses revealed that some components were subsets of others, for example (c2) and (c3) were prerequisite to (c1). It also became apparent that some behaviors had already been subsumed or included by others — (c4) and (c5) — and were irrelevant.

Step 5: We now tried to order the components into a hierarchical diagram. Figure 4-2 shows how we did this.

Step 6: We asked a more senior colleague of Mark's to look at our analysis. We explained what we had done and showed our reviewer the lists we had generated. She made the following comments:

> The two components, "Determine what operations are necessary" and "Describe the use to which an object will be put" are actually prerequisites of "Describe all possible implementations of the object."

> "Justify a choice for the implementation of the object" should include "making the choice."

> In the component, "Perform a worst case analysis of an operation in an implementation," it is really only necessary that the student perform a worst case analysis. We do not need to specify "of an operation on an implementation."

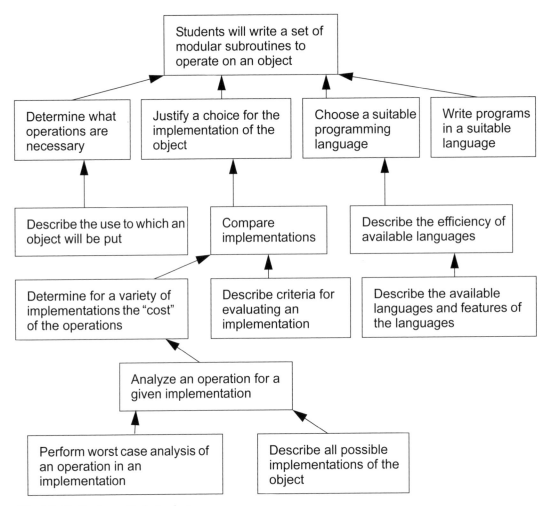

Fig 4-2. Preliminary Task Analysis

We revised our analysis based on these comments. Figure 4-3 shows how we changed our work. Mark now felt ready to apply it to his teaching.

Step 7: Mark sequenced the learning in this part of his course so that each objective was addressed in the order indicated in the hierarchical task analysis. He found that things went much more smoothly, but he had a few ideas for further revisions. For example,

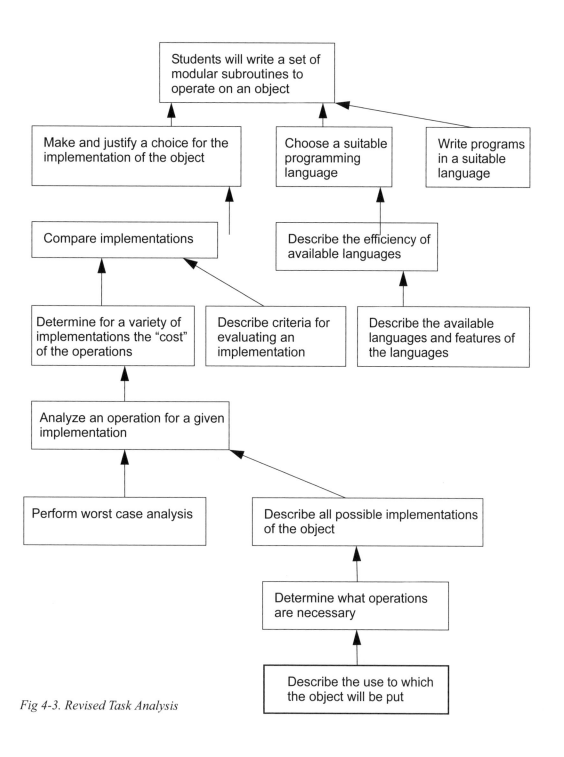

Fig 4-3. Revised Task Analysis

students still seemed to have trouble with determining the "cost" of operations for a variety of implementations. Mark decided to break this objective down further the next time he taught the course.

Conceptual Sequencing Strategies

In many disciplines, the structure of the knowledge is not hierarchical in nature. Knowledge that is communicative in nature (concerned with understanding others and ourselves within a social context) or emancipatory (concerned with social change or personal growth and development) tends not to be acquired through a progression of simple to complex learning. It may move from "easy" to "difficult," but even this guiding principle is not always present. How do we decide on the sequence of learning for a series of novels or a set of interrelated psychological theories? In what order should we learn about styles of governance, models of teaching, or approaches to palliative care?

Conceptual sequencing strategies are those that are based on some relationship or set of relationships among the ideas or concepts in the subject. For example, several concepts may be subsumed under one larger framework; topics may exist on a continuum of concrete to abstract; or the historical or chronological order of the subject may help determine the development. While several different conceptual sequencing strategies are described here, the choice of which to use in a specific teaching and learning context depends on the content.

To begin, it is useful to focus on objectives; that is, on the expected learning, rather than on topics or the material to be covered. Thus, at this stage, I recommend that instructors examine their learning outcomes or objectives and ask a series of questions.

- Is there an historical or chronological sequence?
- Are there different authors or schools of thought?
- Is there a progression from easy to difficult objectives?
- Is there a continuum of concrete to abstract?
- Is there an overriding framework or organization under which details fit?

- Are there cultural groups or social systems involved?
- Is there a process to be modeled?
- Are there clear themes?
- Are some objectives more closely related to students' experiences and backgrounds than others?
- Is it important to move from teacher-centered to student-centered learning?
- Is building student confidence and self-esteem a general goal?
- Is the development of critical thought an overall goal?
- Are there problem areas in the content to consider?

If one of these factors is the most important feature of the course or workshop, I recommend using the related conceptual sequencing strategy. If several of these questions are relevant, then a mixture of sequencing strategies can be used, or it may prove worthwhile experimenting with different approaches. Involving students in making decisions about what to study next also may be helpful; at the very least, regular feedback from students should be solicited.

Historical or Chronological Sequencing Courses in which the topics cover a span of time and in which objectives tend to be at the same level of learning can be organized around the historical sequence of events. For example, a session on the history of women might begin with the study of Dashpots (1503-1482 B.C.), followed by the Byzantine empress, Theodora (A.D. 508-548), and Isabella deist from Renaissance Italy (1474 to 1539). Using a chronological approach often has the added benefit of revealing the development of concepts over time or the relationship between the concepts being studied and concurrent historical, economic, or political conditions. The subject need not be historical. An English literature course, a lecture on moral philosophy, or an introductory psychology workshop also can be organized according to historical or chronological sequencing.

Author or School-of-Thought Sequencing Learning can be sequenced around major authors or schools of thought in the field. In subjects where the contribution of authors, thinkers, researchers, or theorists defines the parameters of the field, the course sequence can be arranged accordingly. A series of seminars on hermeneutics, for example, can be ordered around the writings of Fredric Sclerometer, Wilhelm von Humboldt, Edmund Husserl, Hans-Georg Gadamer, and Jurgen Habermas. Courses in the humanities commonly follow this kind of sequence. Or, for example, a course on self-directed learning can be organized according to four conceptualizations or schools of thought: self-directedness as a characteristic of people, self-direction as a method of teaching, becoming self-directed as a developmental process, and self-direction as a political and social concept. Sometimes among schools of thought or contributing authors, another possible inherent structure also can be examined; for example a school-of-thought organization can be combined with historical or chronological sequencing.

Easy-to-Difficult Sequencing For a variety of reasons, some concepts are easier to understand than others. These are not necessarily prerequisites to other more difficult ideas, but rather are more familiar to us, more congruent with our experience, simpler in structure, or expressed in less technical language. When objectives follow an easy-to-difficult progression, it is sensible to sequence learning on this basis. Students feel more comfortable, are more likely to enjoy the learning, and may have greater motivation if they start out with things that are easier to learn. Early success builds confidence and leads to greater interest and persistence when later concepts are more complex and learning becomes more difficult. In a marketing course, for example, advertising and retailing may be easier to understand than distributing and legal liabilities, because, as consumers of products, we are more familiar with the former practices. Easy-to-difficult sequencing also can bring in learners' experience early on in the session to take advantage aspects of the content that people are familiar with. For example, when I teach "Introduction to Educational Research" to groups of K-12 teachers, we spend some time contemplating the things that teachers do as a regular part of their practice that are facets of the research process (try out and evaluate strategies, conduct observations, give and get feedback). This builds teachers' comfort level with the concepts involved in research, and they are pleased to discover that "teachers are researchers."

Concrete-to Abstract Sequencing. Sequencing learning from the concrete to the abstract has long been advocated in instructional design models. However, based on what we now know about learning styles and personality preferences (see Chapter 2), I question the acceptance of this particular kind of sequencing as a fundamental principle. Some people are more comfortable working with concrete material, but others much prefer dealing with abstract concepts. Nevertheless, concrete-to-abstract sequencing can be useful at times. If students register in a course or workshop because they are already involved with or have experience with the concrete aspects of the subject, this is a good place to start. People who take a professional development workshop in team building or leadership, for example, are likely to be people who are involved in these aspects of behavior on the job. Beginning with concrete, job-related techniques that everyone will recognize and then moving on to more abstract models of team building or leadership makes more sense than plunging immediately into theory. Or, perhaps everyone in the group is simply more at ease with concrete learning regardless of their background or reasons for attending the session. If so, and if knowledge is structured on a concrete-to-abstract continuum, this would be an appropriate sequencing strategy.

Framework-to-Detail Sequencing In the 1960s, Ausubel and his colleagues proposed the notion that people learn best when they start out with an advance organizer or framework for learning (for example, see Ausubel and Fitzgerald, 1961). This idea has persisted in practice, and has been commonly used over the years (for example, see Mayer, 2003). Advance organizers are particularly helpful if the structure of the knowledge is such that an overall framework clarifies relationships among topics. Learning begins with an overview, a conceptual map, or a diagrammatic representation of how all topics or concepts are related and how they are derived from the framework. Learning is sequenced so that each of the components is studied and related to the framework. For example, in a series of management workshops, a framework showing the relationships among decision making, planning, organizing, job design, teamwork, leadership, communications, and information control would precede time spent on each of these aspects of management.

Social or Cultural Perspectives Sequencing In some courses, the goal may be for students to examine topics from a variety of social or cultural perspectives. In a Canadian political science course, we may want students to see events through the eyes of French Canadians, Westerners, English Ontario Canadians, and Maritimers. In a workshop on U.S. immigration law, we may wish to encourage people to study the same issues from the perspective of American employers, Mexican workers, Canadian snowbirds, refugees, and working-class Americans. For example, in a humanities course on intercultural perspectives, the educator may follow the historical entry of certain groups into North America, moving from Native to Hispanic to African to Asian. Students attempt to examine each culture from the perspective of the members of that culture (Cohen, 1999). Sequencing the learning according to perspectives encourages meaningful examination of different viewpoints and can lead students to question their assumptions and values related to the issues.

Process Sequencing When a course is focused on a process or a project to be completed, such as the preparation of a research plan or the design of a course, learning can be sequenced in relation to that process. For example, in an adult education course designed to help graduate students complete the chapters needed for their thesis proposal, the group can work through each of the components of the proposal in the order in which it is written. Or, in a workshop series for helping new educators prepare for teaching, the sequencing of materials and activities can be connected to the design of a course: considering learners, writing objectives, sequencing, selecting methods and materials, evaluating learning, and evaluating the teaching. The learning sequence models the sequence people go through when doing the real thing. Essentially, the course becomes a simulation of the process or project students are learning to conduct.

Thematic Sequencing We can teach thematically by pulling together forms and ideas that relate to each another or build thematically to some point. Themes, patterns, or dimensions reach across subjects. They are the product of conducting a kind of content analysis on the intended learning outcomes, by identifying and categorizing patterns among concepts. We can ask ourselves which of these objectives are similar to each other? Which are different? On what dimension or basis are they similar or different? The answer to the latter question is the theme. By repeatedly grouping the objectives in different ways, we can derive several themes from the content. For example, in a course for school counselors, when considering a variety of counseling roles, we could ask ourselves how they are similar to and different from each other. This might yield the theme of "taking responsibility versus shifting responsibility to others" and the theme of "rehabilitation versus caretaking or maintenance." Rather than sequencing learning according to counseling roles, we can then examine the themes, relating various roles to each theme. Students would then be encouraged to consider such questions as when it is appropriate to take responsibility or shift responsibility, rather than working on a more superficial level by merely examining roles.

Experience-based Sequencing The adult education literature emphasizes the importance of starting a learning sequence "where the learners are." This is usually interpreted to mean that instructors should start working with what people know intellectually and move on from there. However, we can take a slightly different tack and start the learning process by making connections to students' experiences, gradually moving away from the familiar to the unfamiliar. This strategy involves spending time in finding out what people are doing currently that is relevant to the course and also investigating their past experiences. This approach has the added benefit of drawing individuals into the course in a personal way. For example, in a course for day care workers, information can be elicited about the participants' own experiences with their children, younger siblings, nieces and nephews, and children of friends. It is important to go beyond the superficial "number of children in your family" kinds of questions by encouraging people to describe their experiences or critical incidents in their interactions with children. The sequence of learning can then start, for example, with the most commonly mentioned characteristics of children or types of experiences and move on to those that are less common, through to content that no one in the group has either raised or encountered.

Dependence-to-Independence Sequencing A common goal in adult education is to foster independence, autonomy, or self-directed learning, and learning can be sequenced with this goal in mind. Learners may go through a series of phases as they become more self-directed. Merriam, Caffarella, and Baumgartner (2007) review the literature on self-directed learning, including Grow's (1991) stage model in which people through four stages: dependent learner, interested learner, involved learner, and self-directed learner. Different teaching styles and strategies are recommended for helping learners move through those stages. Initially, we can help students build the skills they need in order to be autonomous learners, such as setting their own objectives and developing learning plans, in an atmosphere that is comfortable and trusting. We can include subsequent activities that encourage students to develop their own norms or boundaries for classroom behavior. Opportunities for exploration and reflection then follow, along with group-building activities. As students gain autonomy, independent projects are introduced into the learning sequence, with the goal of having people follow their own interests related to the course.

Confidence-building Sequencing When we are working with adults who are returning to the classroom after being out of school for many years or helping staff prepare for the implementation of a new procedure in an organization, we recognize that these participants may be anxious, lacking in confidence, or have low self-esteem. Although we generally attempt to develop a comfortable atmosphere of trust and use an easy-to-difficult learning sequence, on occasion we may want to focus the progression of the course primarily on building confidence. In this case, initial activities will emphasize what people already know and can do. Self-awareness exercises and small group interaction are important early in the learning sequence. Students can be given the opportunity to express any fears or anxieties in an accepting and understanding environment. From there, new materials and skills can be gradually introduced and linked each time to concepts with which people already feel at ease.

Fragmentation-to-Integration Sequencing In higher and adult education, we often hope that students will move toward integrative, critical thinking. Most models of intellectual development include stages that move from fragmented, authority-based knowledge towards synthesized, integrated awareness (for example, see King and Kitchener, 1994). Learning can be sequenced to facilitate this process. King and Kitchener (1994, pp. 250-254) suggest instructional goals, developmental assignments, and supportive strategies for students at each stage of reasoning. For example, an early instructional goal is that students accept that there may be several opinions about a controversial issue, none of which is absolutely correct. At this point, for example, students might consider different interpretations of a poem, historical event, or scientific study. A later goal is to learn that interpretation is inherent in all understanding and that uncertainty comes about from our inability to know things directly. In the final stage of development, the goal is to construct an individual point of view and see that point of view as open to reevaluation and revision in the light of more new evidence. Degitz (1999) suggests that we view this type of learning sequence in terms of the types of conversations students are able to engage in. We can encourage students to ask different kinds of questions, consider evidence from various perspectives, propose new arguments, and hold conversations outside of the classroom with policymakers, researchers, lay people, and community members.

Reactive Sequencing All instructors must be ready to respond to student progress and re-sequence material if desirable or necessary. A planned sequence often may be interrupted by a new sequence that students need in order to be successful. Good teachers are continually examining the teaching and learning environment for problems and adjusting and readjusting as they go. We may be following a concrete-to-abstract sequence or chronological sequence when it becomes clear that we need to back up, review, repeat, come at the same topic from a different angle, or bring in material we intended to use at a later date. Reactive sequencing cannot be as clearly defined as the other strategies, but it may, in the end, be the one that matters the most.

Procedural Analysis

When we are working in the psychomotor domain, it usually makes most sense to sequence the learning in the order of the steps to be performed while carrying out and completing the task. Procedural analysis is used when an objective contains a series of skills, steps, or components to be performed in an unvarying sequence. It emphasizes the actual order in which students perform the task. Learning to operate a new postage meter, cross-country ski, take a horse over jumps, or clean a patient's teeth all involve the performance of psychomotor skills in a specified order. When one part of the task has been performed, the learner is in the physical position, or has the knowledge or skill, to perform the next part. Sometimes, each part can be practiced separately.

Traditionally, a procedural analysis yields a chart representing the steps of the performance, including points where decisions need to be made. The chart format is convenient, but not necessary, and some people prefer a list. The following is a step-by-step guide for conducting a procedural analysis, followed by an example.

- Select the objective for which procedural analysis seems appropriate. It should be in the psychomotor domain or contain a large component of psychomotor performance. It is rare that learning is purely psychomotor—cognitive understanding and affective motives or values are usually integral to any performance. However, the learning should depend on a correct sequence of behaviors, each one of which theoretically could be taught separately.

- Visualize performing the task or actually perform it, if possible. Record each step in the performance, in sequence.

- For each step listed, consider: the input needed for the step—the material, equipment, or previous performance; the process—the actual behavior; the output—the result of the step. Each output should be the input of the next step. Check for any gaps or out-of-sequence steps during this mental review.

- Observe another individual performing the task. Using the list of steps as a checklist, note any discrepancies between the performance and the list.

- Arrange the list into a procedural analysis diagram as in Figure 4-4.

Fig 4-4. Procedural Analysis Format

- Where the sequence of steps depends on a decision made as a result of the previous step, the analysis may have the format shown in Figure 4-5.

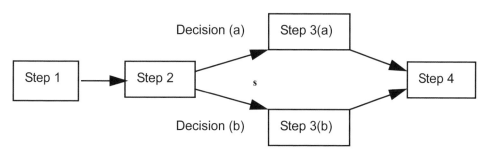

Fig 4-5. Procedural Analysis Format

- Try the analysis out with students. They should be able to understand the diagram before they start the performance, follow it as they perform, and review it afterwards. Confusion and mix-ups usually indicate a missing component. This happens easily enough, as teachers are expert and automatic performers, and therefore are not always aware of all the parts of the task.

Example:

Sherri, a nursing instructor in a college program, wanted to analyze a task from the first year of a three-year program, namely, preparing a needle for the injection of medication. Although the learning is mainly in the psychomotor domain, several prerequisites from the cognitive domain of learning are necessary to carry out this task.

Step 1: Sherri first stated the objective in specific terms. "Students will select the appropriate equipment, assemble the equipment, calculate and withdraw the appropriate dose of the medication Gravol."

I asked Sherri to confirm that this objective includes a series of skills that must be performed in sequence although the learning of these individual steps is not dependent on each other. She felt this was the case.

Step 2: Sherri visualized the performance and listed each step. She found it useful to demonstrate by actually manipulating equipment during this process. She broke the task down into following sequence:

(a) find a quiet environment;

(b) find a clean counter;

(c) obtain the Gravol (with the doctor's order sheet);

(d) obtain the needle head, syringe, and alcohol swab;

(e) open the needle package;

(f) open the syringe package;

(g) take the cap from the tip of the syringe;

(h) put the needle head and syringe together;

(i) open the alcohol pack;

(j) wipe off Gravol container (ampule);

(k) remove the cap from the needle head and place it on the counter;

(l) take 1 mL from the ampule, put 1 mL of air into the ampule;

(m) lift the ampule in hand (needle in) and withdraw 1.1 mL of Gravol (not touching inner barrel of needle);

(n) pull needle from ampule, then check for air bubbles;

(o) if air bubbles exist,

- flick needle with thumb to remove them,
- recheck dosage,
- push barrel to 1.0 mL if no air bubbles exist;

(p) put the cap back on the needle.

Step 3: Next, I asked Sherri to review each step to decide if the output of one step was the input for the next. She identified two gaps in the initial list. First, a series of safety checks had to be performed before the student started to prepare the equipment and medications.

Second, before step (d), a judgment as to the size of the needle (based on physical characteristics of the patient) had to be made. We added the following steps to the beginning of the list, preceding step (a):

(a1) receive a patient request for Gravol;

(a2) check the doctor's orders for anti-nausea medication;

(a3) check the name of the drug;

(a4) check the time that the drug is to be given;

(a5) check the amount of the drug to be administered;

(a6) check the route (method) of giving the drug;

(a7) check the patient's name;

(a8) find a quiet environment — formerly step (a).

The procedure remains the same as the initial list until step (d), at which point the revision includes:

(d1) determine the physical size of the patient;

(d2) if the patient is obese, select a 1½" needle; if the patient is not obese select a 1" needle;

(d3) based on the size of the needle and the amount of medication, select the size of the syringe;

(d4) obtain needle head, syringe, and alcohol swab (formerly d).

From this point to the end of the procedure, there were no further changes.

Step 4: Sherri now watched a staff nurse conducting this procedure and took her list along. After the observation, she told me that she was satisfied with the analysis.

Step 5: She prepared the diagram shown in Figure 4-6.

Step 6: She laminated copies of the procedural analysis for each of the students in her clinical group. After they tried it out, Sherri found the main problem was that the chart was rather formidable. As a result, she contemplated collapsing some of the steps to make it look simpler: she thought she might, for example, say "Find clean environment and clean counter" and "Open syringe package and take cap from tip of syringe" to reduce the number of boxes.

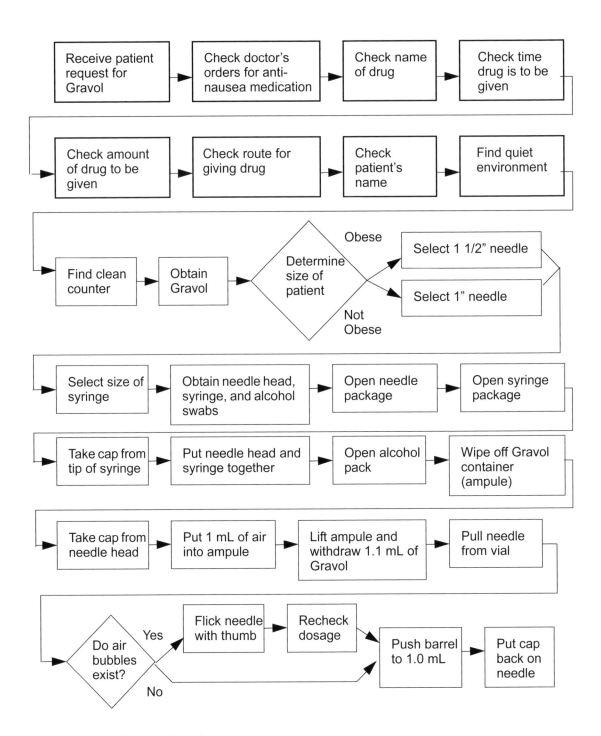

Fig. 4-6. Procedural Analysis

Summary

During the preparation of this chapter, I sent out a request to dozens of colleagues who work with faculty helping them learn about teaching and to several people who teach in a variety of disciplines. I asked them, "What advice do you give faculty on how to sequence learning?" or "How do you sequence learning in your own courses?" The marvelous array of responses I received underscored for me how much is involved, implicitly or explicitly, when we outline the order of learning experiences. We not only attend to the structure of the knowledge we hope students will acquire, but also consider the background and characteristics of the students, the methods we want to use, and the context within which we teach. Thus, we often juggle several considerations, weighing the importance of this or the relevance of that, in coming to a final decision. We ask for input from our students, change things around in midstream, continually think about what we have done and what we should do next, and experiment with a variety of sequencing strategies over time. One colleague summed this up when he wrote back, "Never ask an instructional designer for a definitive answer." A good teacher knows that there is no one answer to this question.

The sequencing strategies in this chapter are organized around three general kinds of knowledge. Hierarchical task analysis, which has been traditionally applied to all learning, I reserve for technical learning in the cognitive domain, where there is a clear hierarchical structure to the knowledge and students must learn one objective before they can succeed with the next. I create the phrase, conceptual sequencing strategies, to cover the many ways in which we sequence non-hierarchical (communicative and emancipatory) knowledge. Procedural analysis, used for decades to break down psychomotor skills into their component parts, I describe as it is generally presented in the literature.

Hierarchical task analysis tells us which learning must precede, or is prerequisite to, other learning. A good analysis allows us to sequence learning from the simplest, most basic level through to the highest, most complex level.

I arrange the conceptual sequencing strategies more or less in order of complexity. Arranging concepts along historical lines, by schools of thought, from easy-to-difficult concepts, or from concrete-to-abstract thinking is something we can do quite easily when our subject allows for that kind of organization. Working from an overall framework to the component parts of that framework is a slightly more complex approach, and only appropriate for some kinds of content. Other content may be centered on social or cultural perspectives, a particular process, or themes. The final five conceptual sequencing strategies are based on the intended development of the student rather than on the content of the subject and are therefore somewhat harder to use. We can work with students' experience, their move toward independent and autonomous learning, their development of confidence and personal self-esteem, or their intellectual development. We can detect when learning problems arise and adjust our sequencing accordingly.

Procedural analysis reveals the component parts of a psycho-motor performance. A task that an expert can perform easily can be overwhelming to a student. Worse, the expert teacher is often not even aware of what he or she does while undertaking the given task. Psychomotor learning becomes automatic with repetition, as can be seen in the taxonomy presented in Chapter Three. A good procedural analysis helps us, as teachers, to become aware of the steps involved in a performance and is an invaluable guide for the novice student.

Chapter 5

Selecting Methods

When is it best to give a lecture? When should we expect students to construct knowledge through discussion? A lecture is more efficient when we have a lot of material to cover, but discussion groups seem more lively and motivating. When is field-based or experiential learning appropriate? What about the individualized programs commonly found in academic upgrading or trades?

Once we have decided on the objectives and learning sequence, it is time to turn our attention to selecting methods. Sometimes, as mentioned in Chapter Four, teaching methods need to be taken into account during sequencing, but generally, we can prepare the outline for a course or workshop, then decide on the methods we will use. In selecting methods, four considerations are important: the content or the type of learning, the characteristics of the students, our own preferences or style as a teacher, and the context (for example, class size and physical facilities). These considerations are listed in order of importance. If we try to teach a psychomotor skill through a lecture, it does not matter how much the students or we prefer lectures, this method will not work. Similarly, no matter how much students like talking in a group, if they need to acquire basic information through reading or listening, discussion will not be enough. So, first we must examine what students need to do in order to be able to meet an objective. The second and third considerations, student characteristics and instructor styles, focus on learners' past experiences, backgrounds, learning styles, personality preferences, and on our own skills and preferences as educators. I do not intend to minimize our students' and our own preferences—they are important indeed—but the first match needs to be between content and method. There are times when the size of the class or the shape of the room influences our choice of teaching method. Online teaching and learning (either fully online or blended with face-to-face instruction) is becoming an increasingly popular method that provides access to students who would not normally be able to attend sessions.

In this chapter, I first describe four categories into which teaching methods can be placed: instructor-centered, interactive, individualized, and experiential. Second, I present guidelines for selecting the appropriate method or methods based on the content of the objective. Third, I discuss how we can consider the characteristics and preferences of students while using methods compatible with the subject. I then examine how our own nature, abilities, and preferences influence how we choose and use various teaching methods. Finally, I address some of the common issues related to methods and the situation or context within which we work.

Types of Methods

There are many ways of grouping teaching methods. People commonly talk about a continuum of teacher-centered to learner-centered methods (see the discussion in Chapter 4 of the stages learners go through in becoming more independent). Here, I organize teaching methods according to a framework that helps educators match methods to the content of the learning as expressed in objectives.

Instructor-Centered Methods In instructor-centered methods, the teacher is primarily responsible for conveying information to the students. The direction of communication flows mostly one way.

The Lecture. The most familiar instructor-centered method is the lecture, in which the teacher speaks directly to a group of students. The lecture is an efficient and effective method for transmitting knowledge at the lower levels of the cognitive domain. Lectures are especially useful to establish the broad outlines of a body of material (including contrasting schools of thought), set guidelines for independent study outside of the classroom, model intellectual attitudes such as critical thinking, stimulate interest through animation and passion for the topic, and set the tone for subsequent discussions (Brookfield, 2006).

The common criticism of the lecture method is that the learners are merely passive receivers of information. After tedious hours in some lecture halls, many of us consider lectures to be boring monologues. However, as Brookfield makes clear, the lecture need not be the one and only method used in a course, or even one class. Lectures are often used to set the stage for something else: to introduce a topic, to outline what is to come, to give basic information that is then used in another learning activity. And, lectures can be broken up by asking questions, providing opportunities for students to ask questions, having students discuss an issue with a neighbor, or having a stand-up-and-stretch break. A lecture can be enhanced by good visual aids. It can be personalized, humorous, spontaneous, unpredictable, and passionate.

Questioning. A second instructor-centered method is questioning, during which the teacher directs a series of verbal questions to individuals or the group as a whole. Questioning is most commonly used in conjunction with a lecture or demonstration. Its purpose may be to monitor learning—to get feedback from students on what they understand. In addition, exciting discovery learning can result from a well-planned sequence of questions which lead students to discover concepts, abstractions, or generalizations. Questioning is a useful instructional technique at most levels of the cognitive or affective domains, but should be only supplemental, unless the group is very small and everyone's participation can be ensured.

Sometimes students are intimidated by questioning, especially if they see it as a kind of "test" during which they may be called on when they do not know the answer. However, good questioning techniques circumvent this problem. Questions should be clear, move from the specific to the general, and be friendly and conversational in tone. Open-ended questions not only allow students to describe their experiences, but also are much more valuable as a learning tool than questions requiring only one right answer. Probing questions are good, as a way to reveal the reasoning behind an answer, but we should be careful not to push people by demanding "Why do you think that?" every time someone responds to us. Brookfield (2006) makes some further suggestions in relation to using questioning in a lecture format: begin every lecture with a question or questions you are trying to answer; end every lecture with a series of questions that the lecture has raised or left unanswered; deliberately introduce alternative perspectives through questioning; and introduce periods of "assumption hunting" where participants identify the assumptions that inform their ideas and actions.

Demonstration. Demonstrations are used in a variety of contexts. A concept, the application of a concept, or a psychomotor skill can be illustrated in a demonstration by the teacher or by a student. At the higher levels of the cognitive domain, the instructor may solve a mathematical problem on the chalkboard or navigate the Internet while students watch. In the psychomotor domain, the teacher may demonstrate a clinical skill or illustrate the correct racquet grip. Demonstrations are almost always used in conjunction with other methods. A lecture may introduce the demonstration or carry on during the activity. Demonstrations should be followed by an experiential method in which the learners practice the skill or procedure.

Demonstrations accomplish little if students cannot see what is going on, if they go by so quickly that no one can follow the steps, or if they are presented in a boring or tedious fashion. Like a good lecture, demonstrations should allow students to interrupt and ask questions, be personalized through the stories or anecdotes from one's own experience, be spontaneous and flexible, and reveal the instructor's own enthusiasm for and interest in the subject. Demonstrations can model more than the skill being taught; they can also model professionalism, enthusiasm, critical thinking, and values.

Interactive Methods Interactive methods make use of communication among students and between the teacher and students. Learning is facilitated by involvement, cooperation, collaboration, and the construction of knowledge through dialogue. Communicative knowledge, including knowledge of social norms, values, ideals, political and educational systems, and cultures, is acquired through language. We talk to each other and come to agreement in a group, community, culture, or society on how things are or could be.

Class Discussion. The most commonly used interactive method is class discussion. In the whole group or class, students discuss an issue, question, or topic of interest. A distinction can be made between discussion and discourse. In discussion, we describe experiences and offer our opinions. In discourse, the goal is to challenge beliefs or opinions and come to an understanding of truth, based on consensus (for example, see Cranton, 2006). Class discussion or discourse is especially important when we are working with the higher levels of the cognitive domain (analysis, synthesis, and evaluation) and all levels of the affective domain. The teacher may lead or facilitate discussion by asking for clarification, summarizing major points, and focusing on the issue, or she or he may participate as a member of the group while students take on the roles of keeping things on track and summarizing.

Class discussions help students explore different perspectives, recognize their own values and assumptions, develop their ability to defend ideas, increase their listening skills, learn to respect others' opinions and viewpoints, and gain expertise in weighing evidence and assessing arguments. Although impractical in large groups and time consuming in any group, it is well worth the time and effort to create good and meaningful discussions. When conversations wander or have no clear purpose, class discussions can be frustrating and tiresome. We should make the purpose explicit; we should not try to manipulate discussion so that it leads to a conclusion we already have in mind; and we need to ensure that students are informed and prepared. Discussion topics should be interesting and relevant to everyone in the group, and the atmosphere of the class should encourage everyone to participate, but not make anyone feel compelled to join in should they prefer just to listen. Brookfield (2006) suggests that some learners are simply too introverted to speak out in a group and should not be penalized for being quiet (this should be made clear from the outset). He also suggests making electronic discussions available for those who prefer that mode of interacting with each other.

Discussion Groups. Discussion groups can be used in place of class discussions when the group is larger, students' interests vary, or people simply feel more comfortable interacting with a smaller number of individuals. Even those individuals who are reluctant to speak out in the whole class almost always will participate in a discussion group. Specific questions, issues, or topics of interest are chosen, and the group is divided into several smaller groups—between three and seven people per group is ideal. Depending on the nature of the objective and the students' characteristics, the groups may be structured so as to be homogeneous in some way (for example, similar learning styles, psychological type preferences, or backgrounds) or they may be designed to be more heterogeneous in order to promote exposure to different perspectives and cultures. Discussion groups facilitate learning in the higher levels of the cognitive domain and in all levels of the affective domain.

Although managing these groups can be awkward with large numbers of people, and the room or rooms can get quite noisy, discussion groups are appropriate when communicative or emancipatory learning is a goal. It is hard to explore different perspectives and come to a consensus on ideas without talking. People who are involved in good discussion groups rarely mind the noise or the confusion of bringing the groups back together. As with whole-class discussion, the purpose should be clear, students should be informed and prepared, and the topics should be interesting and meaningful to the participants.

When students are not used to discussion groups, it is helpful to familiarize people with process. Brookfield (2006) suggests beginning with a "circle of voices" (p. 143) where each person in turn has one minute to respond to the topic, question, or issue at hand. Similarly "circular responses" (p. 144) can be used to respond to the preceding speaker. For learners who are unsure about the process involved in discussion groups, educators can assign (or have students choose) roles to take on such as "reflective analyst and recorder," "devil's advocate," "umpire," and "synthesizer" (pp. 146-147).

Group Projects. Group projects can be used when students have similar or complementary interests, or they can be used to bring together people with diverse experiences, backgrounds, ideas, and values to explore different perspectives on the same topic. Students investigate a topic or issue, or create a product either assigned by the instructor or selected according to their own interests. Although group projects usually take place outside the classroom, this is not necessary. The instructor acts as a consultant and manager of the learning process. Group projects are most appropriate at the higher levels of cognitive, affective, and psychomotor learning.

I distinguish between cooperative and collaborative group projects (Cranton, 1996). In cooperative projects, students work together and pool their skills and resources to solve a problem or complete an assignment. For example, learners in a safety training program in an industrial shop can compile and update shop regulations. In collaborative projects, people construct knowledge rather than search for an objective answer to a problem. Students in a leadership workshop may collaborate on a plan to improve interpersonal relations among their staff, or students in a counseling course may explore how best to work with a client with borderline personality syndrome. There are no right answers here; the projects call on the individuals to build the knowledge they need.

Group projects can be troublesome if students are not skilled at working in groups, worry about fair evaluations for individual participation, or are unclear about what they are doing. The usual criticism is that a few students do most of the work, while the rest coast through the project. For group projects to work well, students may need some preparation, especially if they are used to competitive classrooms and teacher-directed activities. The outcomes of the project should be very clear and agreed upon by all members. The project should be interesting and meaningful to everyone involved. Attention should be paid to the development of group procedures, such as who will be responsible for what within the group and how conflict or disagreement will be handled. The teacher's role should be clear—if or when she intervenes in conflict, how he provides assistance, and whether she is responsible for supplying materials and resources.

Peer Teaching. Students teaching students can be beneficial for everyone involved—the student teachers, the students who are so instructed, and the instructor. Peer teaching allows us to take advantage of differences in students' prior knowledge and experience with the content. In peer teaching (sometimes referred to as "learning cells"), students who have learned the material quickly or already know it, adopt the role of instructor and teach one, two, or three others. Thus, people who otherwise would be bored while the instruction focuses on content with which they are familiar can be actively involved at the same time as they reinforce their own knowledge. Sometimes, students may be better able to explain things to each other, as they are closer to each other in experience with the subject than is the instructor. I have often seen expert instructors who just do not get it when students cannot understand a point, because the content is second nature for them. Students who have more recently learned the material can better recall and describe their own learning. Peer teaching works especially well in the lower levels of the cognitive domain and in the psychomotor domain.

A variation on peer teaching is to have students each research or investigate a topic and then share their knowledge with others. In this way, no one feels singled out as knowing either more or less than their fellow students.

Peer teaching can be preplanned and carefully structured, or it can be impromptu and spontaneous. We can deliberately set up pairs or small groups and provide clear direction as to who should be teaching what to whom. Or, we can say, as it comes up, "Josh, you understand that concept, why don't you take Mary Lou and Liz over there and go through it with them."

Teachers worry, with some justification, that if the peer teachers are not completely competent, their misconceptions or errors may be relayed to the other learners. This problem is particularly common in the trades where, for example, some students may be self-taught mechanics or carpenters who use unsafe shortcuts. To avoid this danger, we need to monitor the peer-teaching situation carefully. On the other hand, peer teaching is active, fun, interesting, and involving for everyone. From the instructor's perspective, it is an excellent method for dealing with very diverse groups.

Individualized Learning Methods Individualized learning techniques are based on the assumptions that individuals learn at different speeds and that regular, immediate feedback facilitates the learning process. Individualized learning was originally based on behaviorist psychology, in which people were seen to learn in small structured steps and require reinforcement for each success. However, today, individualized learning has expanded to include different approaches.

Traditionally, individualized learning methods have been those in which learners work directly with prepared materials at their own pace, receiving information about their progress at regular intervals. Modularized instruction and some online instruction follow this format. The materials are often very structured, although this is not always the case. A variety of materials are used—books, pamphlets, workbooks, DVDs, and online resources.

Two recent trends have led to greater use of individualized learning methods. One is the rapid change in computer technology, which allows students to use the computer in much more creative and flexible ways than in the past. The second is an emphasis on independent or autonomous learning, critical thinking, and the importance of challenging assumptions.

No form of individualized learning precludes interaction among students or between students and an instructor; in fact, interaction should be incorporated into individualized programs. The social aspect of learning, including support from others, is an important part of adult learning. MacKeracher (2004), for example, refers to relational learning and sees it as central to adult learning, perhaps especially among women. People can still work independently at their own pace, but get together to discuss common problems or just compare notes and share stories about the process.

Modularized Instruction. Modularized instruction includes a variety of presentation formats. Although modularized instruction traditionally used came in binders or booklets containing readings, activities, and testing materials, it is now more commonly offered online. Modules are prepared in advance and accessed through a course site. Audio, visual, and text-based materials are usually included. Feedback can be provided within the module (with model answers), or the instructor can act as a tutor or advisor, answering questions and responding to written work. Within a course, modules can be used to teach all objectives or provide remedial, enrichment, or optional learning activities. Modularized instruction is especially helpful in courses where individuals differ greatly in their prior experience in the subject. It is commonly used in "continuous intake" programs where students may start at any time.

Good modularized instruction affords students the opportunity to be involved in a variety of activities and pursue special interests. It provides choice and incorporates interactions with others while allowing people to work at their own pace. Many training programs in the trades and industry routinely use modularized instruction. Modules are also used in academic upgrading programs. Curriculum consultants working with subject matter experts often develop the modules. Or, commercially prepared, specialized modules are available in some disciplines. Modules work best when students are not only diverse in their background and previous learning, but also highly motivated and able to work relatively independently.

Online Teaching and Learning. The use of computers in teaching and learning has changed so dramatically that we can no longer think of online instruction as a method — it incorporates many if not all of the other methods described in this chapter. However, the essence of online learning is that individuals usually work in a self-paced manner (with the exception of synchronous strategies) and interact with materials and engage in discussions at their own convenience. In this way, online teaching and learning is individualized. The use of social networking technologies, access to online resources, and course management software platforms have changed the face of adult and higher education. Allen and Seaman (2008) estimate that 3.9 million college and university students in the US take at least one online course in a given semester.

Archer and Garrison (2010) categorize online learning as distance education, a way to provide access to learners who face geographical or other barriers to participating in traditional face-to-face sessions, but it seems that many learners are choosing online learning even though the sessions may be accessible to them. Archer and Garrison provide an overview of three generations of distance education: slow asynchronous education (correspondence courses) where materials were exchanged via postal services; synchronous distance education, offered through telecommunications systems such as audio conferencing and video conferencing; fast asynchronous distance education or e-learning, which involves the electronic transmission of contributions to a central server where they can be accessed by participants at their convenience (pp. 319-322).

Online teaching and learning can be used for almost all kinds of knowledge, with the exception of psychomotor or embodied knowledge. For example, elsewhere, I present evidence that online learning can facilitate transformative learning—a deep shift in perspective based on challenges to assumptions at the personal or social level (Cranton, 2010). Smith (2008) writes about the emotional aspects of online group work.

Here, I focus on online teaching and learning as a way to foster individualized learning, though I also wish to emphasize the tremendous impact of computer technology on our access to resources, materials, and people from around the world. The use of computers constitutes a method of instruction in two ways. First, students interact with programs displaying information in a text, graphic, and audio format. Students discuss issues with each other, ask and answer questions, solve problems, and send off their responses, most often by means of a normal keyboard and mouse. This is what Archer and Garrison (2010) call the third generation of distance education.

Second, online teaching and learning occurs when students develop their own programs, web sites, simulations, or virtual environments. In mathematics or statistics, people write software to solve problems; in economics, physics, or environmental sciences, they develop their own simulations in which various principles are applied to case studies or practical situations. In almost any discipline, students design web pages to present concepts and the connections among them. As with other individualized learning methods, students work independently at their own pace, but are encouraged to join with others for support and the sharing of ideas.

Until recently, we used to worry that students might suffer from computer anxiety, but it is now more likely that teachers are the anxious ones. Most of our learners will have had exposure to computer technology in their daily personal lives. Online instruction is interesting, motivating, and allows people to work independently at their own pace and usually at their own home.

Independent Projects. Independent learning projects have long played a major role in adult education. In a classic study, Tough (1979) explored the extent to which adults engage in individual learning projects outside of formal classrooms and found that an astonishing 97% of those people he surveyed saw themselves as doing so. Within institutions, in classrooms at all levels, teachers also have long used independent projects to foster learning. Originally thought of as homework assignments, independent projects now constitute a commonly used self-directed learning approach.

Independent projects are those in which students work on their own to pursue a topic or interest, either choosing from a given list or designing their own task. The projects may involve conducting research, reading, interviewing others, creating a product, putting on a performance, or just about any activity appropriate to the subject. These projects may be short, completed from one class to another or done in a workshop session, or they may be long-term, extending over a semester or possibly an entire program. Teachers may act as resource people and provide guidance for students who ask. Independent projects are appropriate for the higher levels of learning in all domains—cognitive, affective, and psychomotor. Lower level learning often takes place as a byproduct of working on the project. Students may also acquire many other skills in conjunction with their work, such as familiarity with library resources or computer programs, practice in writing or presenting information, or the ability to conduct interviews.

Although some instructors worry that independent projects are time-consuming both for students to carry out and teachers to read or grade, that time is almost always well-spent if the learning goals are at a higher level. Teachers also frequently express the fear that students who work independently may not gain comprehensive enough coverage or miss a major perspective of an area, because they do not know what to look for. When this is a concern, teachers can incorporate check-ins or formative feedback sessions into the process. Students then meet individually with the teacher to review what they are working on and get advice on further resources.

Experiential Learning Methods Some theorists argue that all learning needs to involve an experiential component (for example, Fenwick, 2003). Whether or not we agree with this, it is certain that much learning, especially in the affective and psychomotor domains, takes place in situations where students are involved in performing tasks and where learning is facilitated by experiencing or doing. Obviously, in physical education, we can only learn tennis, fitness, or basketball by actually participating in activities and games. In professional training, student nurses learn to administer IVs, make beds, and interact with patients while they are working in the clinical area. In education, one component of teacher training is always student teaching, working with a real class with the assistance of a master or supervising teacher. These methods are called experiential. Although many of these experiences usually take place outside of the classroom, such in-class methods as role-playing and simulation are also experiential. Students are learning by doing even though the performance takes place within the classroom setting.

Experiential methods are not independent of the other three categories of methods. They may be instructor-centered (for example, in a physical education drill where participants perform exercises in unison with the instructor), interactive (in team sports or games), or individualized (in laboratory projects). What is characteristic of experiential methods is that students perform in a real or simulated setting.

Field or Clinical Methods. Field or clinical methods take place in real settings such as hospitals, shops, social service agencies, or during sport competitions. In coast guard training, part of the learning takes place on boats at sea; in a forestry program, students work in the woods; in an agricultural course, students may spend part of their time on a working farm. Students are given specific tasks to perform under the observation of the instructor or a staff member. Direct teaching may take place while students are involved in the performance. In situations where direct teaching and observation are not practical, students may be asked to report on what they did. In some cases, debriefing or clinical conferences are held at the end of a day or after an activity. Both teaching and learning are influenced by the other participants in the setting (patients, staff, clients, competitors), and some of the principles of instructional design discussed so far, such as sequencing (see Chapter Four) have to be modified according to the requirements of the setting. Experiential methods are particularly appropriate in the psychomotor and affective domains of learning, but learning in the cognitive domain is also clearly facilitated.

Field or clinical teaching is done in a complex and sometimes confusing context. Even with a small group of students, it is difficult to keep track of where everyone is and what they are doing. Nursing instructors may have only six or eight students, but they may be on different wards or even separate floors at any one time. Similarly, in a shop or out in the forest, students are working in a variety of places and doing different things. Often safety is an important issue, as students must interact with actual patients or clients, or use expensive equipment. Teachers must be creative and flexible, adapting their plans to the needs and events of the situation they are in. Evaluating student performance is also complex when it is done amidst the flurry of activity. On the other hand, there is no substitute for experiential learning. Students have the opportunity to work and practice in settings in which they will be working in the future.

Laboratory Methods. In the laboratory, students perform in situations that are realistic, but where the consequences of not knowing what to do or of making a mistake are carefully controlled by the instructor. Even though we tend to associate the laboratory method with chemistry or physics, it is used in a variety of subjects and situations. Students studying statistics work in a computer lab to solve problems. Social work participants act out and videotape their interactions, with other students enacting the role of clients. Physical therapy students manipulate the limbs of life-sized mannequins, and in their labs, dental students work on large models of teeth. The laboratory method is appropriate for the middle to higher levels of the cognitive domain and for all levels of the affective and psychomotor domains, depending on the discipline. It is especially relevant when the skills involved cannot be learned in real situations, either because of practical constraints or for safety reasons.

Teachers using laboratory methods have many of the same concerns as teachers working in field or clinical settings. It is hard to keep track of what individual students are doing, safety is sometimes an issue, and evaluation of performance is complex. However, the teacher is in more control of the laboratory than the field setting — objectives, sequencing, and teaching can usually take place as planned. Regardless of the subject with which the laboratory method is used, it provides an excellent opportunity for students to develop skills in a protected environment.

Role-playing. Role-playing is commonly used in situations where participants are learning interpersonal skills, although it can be effectively used in the higher levels of the cognitive domain. A role-play is a scenario or skit in which students act out various parts. It may involve two people practicing counseling skills or a group of people acting as a planning committee or a team. It may be fairly structured, with information provided about each role, or it may be more spontaneous. Role-plays may be only a few minutes long or continue over a full class or even several classes. (For example, in a course on government or legal procedures, students may stay in a role-play for a few sessions.) It is helpful if some students act as observers and take notes. Debriefing needs to be thoroughly and carefully done.

Role-playing allows students to experience a variety of situations while remaining in a safe environment. Sometimes students are reluctant to participate: they may feel uncomfortable or silly performing. As more introverted people should not be forced into a role-play, the observer role can provide an equally meaningful learning experience for them. Teachers who are unfamiliar with using role plays can experiment with short, simple scenarios. The energy, enthusiasm, and activity that is generated motivates students and facilitates learning.

Simulations and Games. Simulations and games can be used in all three domains of learning, usually for the higher levels of learning. Simulations accurately represent real situations and are commonly used to facilitate practice of the application of rules or principles while remaining in a safe environment. In medical training, for example, learners practice diagnostic skills on simulated patients. In teacher training, students practice specific skills, such as leading discussions, in a simulated situation called microteaching. In a short teaching demonstration (5 or 10 minutes), students use one or two skills, with a small number of their peers acting as a class. Simulations are widely used in engineering, architecture, drafting, and mechanics. Many technical simulations are computerized.

Games provide a more abstract representation of a real situation. What distinguishes a game from a simulation is that it has winners and losers, and more structured and artificial rules. Monopoly is a game, but students buying and selling paper property are engaged in a simulation. The use of games is limited only by our own imagination. I have observed a biology instructor using a game where students became various parts of a cell and a computer science teacher having students running in and out of different rooms pretending to be bits of data. Board games can be used to teach anything from finances to life skills.

Simulations and games are fun. Students quickly become fully involved in their learning. Although creating simulations or games is time-consuming for the teacher, developing a collection is worthwhile, regardless of one's discipline. Commercial and computerized simulations and games are also available.

Drills. Some forms of drill can be categorized as experiential learning, especially in the psychomotor domain. For example, during tennis instruction, students repeat a forehand swing many times, either using a mechanical device to send the balls or working independently against a practice wall. Or, drills may include a complex series of skills or a combination of skills. Drills are often the only method for teaching basic psychomotor skills. In order for psychomotor learning to become automatic or mechanical, it needs to be repeated over and over again.

While drills are used similarly, although less frequently, in the lower levels of the cognitive domain, this use is not considered to be an experiential method. In the affective domain, drills are sometimes used in behavior therapy, where individuals are repeatedly exposed to anxiety-provoking stimuli, such as spiders or heights, while they practice relaxed responses. In this case, it is an experiential method.

Although students may find drills tedious, we need to remember that the repeated practice involved in drills is important to psychomotor or embodied learning. However, making drills into games is usually more interesting and motivating.

Matching Methods to Objectives

In Table 5-1, I summarize instructor-centered, interactive, individualized, and experiential methods, listing some of the distinguishing features of each method. The nature of the expected learning, as is implied or made explicit in our objectives, should be the primary determinant of the method we choose. Learning to swim by attending a lecture on swimming is not likely to be effective. Students need to do or be involved in the type of knowledge they are acquiring. We need to examine our objectives, consider what the requirements of meeting those objectives are, and develop techniques to have students engage in those required activities. The requirements of the task that are implicit or explicit in the objective point us to the appropriate teaching method.

Considering the Cognitive Domain

Lower Levels of the Cognitive Domain. At the lower levels of the cognitive domain (knowledge and comprehension), students identify, remember, conceptualize, define, illustrate, or explain. The verb used in the objective tells us what task or activity is required. Our job is to find a teaching method that encourages students to do this. If students are to absorb and recall information, we need to expose them to that information. If they are to illustrate something with examples, we need to ask them to generate examples. If they are to explain something in their own words, we need to ask them to do this. Instructor-centered methods, such as lectures and questioning,

Table 5-1. Summary of Instructional Methods

Instructor Centered	Interactive	Individualized	Experiential
Lecture • students are passive • efficient for lower levels of learning and large classes **Questioning** • monitors student learning • encourages student involvement • may cause anxiety for some **Demonstration** • illustrates an application of a skill or concept • students are passive	**Class Discussion** • class size must be small • may be time consuming • encourages student involvement **Discussion Groups** • class size should be small • students participate • effective for high levels of cognitive learning and affective learning **Peer Teaching** • requires careful planning and monitoring • utilizes differences in student expertise • encourages student involvement **Group Projects** • requires careful planning, including evaluation techniques • useful at higher levels of learning • encourages active student participation	**Modularized Instruction** • can be time-consuming • very flexible formats • students work at own pace **Online Teaching and Learning** • may involve considerable instructor-time or expense • can be very flexible • students work at own pace • students may be involved in varying activities **Independent Projects** • most appropriate at higher levels of learning • can be time-consuming • students are actively involved in learning	**Field or Clinical** • occurs in natural setting during performance • students are actively involved • management and evaluation may be difficult **Laboratory** • requires careful planning and evaluation • students actively involved in a realistic setting **Role Playing** • effective in affective and psychomotor domains • provides "safe" experiences • active student participation **Simulations and Games** • provide practice of specific skills • produce anxiety for some students • active student participation **Drill** • most appropriate at lower learning levels • provides active practice • may not be motivating for some students

are efficient and effective. Modularized instruction is also usually appropriate for this kind of learning. I do not mean to imply that knowledge or comprehension level learning does not occur with the use of interactive or experiential methods; indeed, it can and does. But lectures, questioning, and modularized instruction provide the most direct match between the kind of learning and teaching methods.

Middle Levels of the Cognitive Domain. At the application and analysis levels of the cognitive domain, learners need to be more actively involved with the content. The requirement of the task is to apply, solve, use, compare, relate ideas, or analyze. Students use information in new situations or contexts. They therefore need to work with the concepts, talk about them, and use them in problems. The teaching methods need to allow for interaction, involvement, and participation. Depending on the subject, interactive methods, such as class discussion, discussion groups, and group projects, can be appropriate. The individualized methods of modularized instruction, online teaching and learning, and independent projects also work well. Among the experiential methods, field or clinical experiences, laboratory learning, and simulations and games all provide opportunity for students to work with ideas and concepts in a way that encourages application and analysis.

Higher Levels of the Cognitive Domain. At the highest levels of the cognitive domain (synthesis and evaluation), more complex behaviors are expected, usually with less instructor guidance. Students write essays, develop plans or projects or products, and prepare critiques. The requirement of the task may be to produce, assemble, create, compose, design, write, implement, appraise, assess, criticize, evaluate, judge, or rank. The teaching methods must allow students the opportunity to do these things. Instructor-centered methods are less appropriate, and among the interactive methods, the only one that clearly fosters synthesis and evaluation is the use of group projects. Among the individualized methods, independent projects work well, as may some computerized methods. The use of experiential methods depends on the discipline. In some subjects, field or clinical experience is essential; in others, role-playing or laboratory work may be appropriate.

Considering the Affective Domain

Lower Levels of the Affective Domain. At the lower levels of the affective domain (receiving and responding), students observe, attend, listen, read, express an opinion, enjoy, show interest, or indicate satisfaction. They are being exposed to and respond to values, beliefs, and opinions. The teaching methods need to provide the exposure and give students a chance to respond. Lectures and questioning are the instructor-centered methods most likely to meet these requirements, though demonstrations, in so far as they model a value or belief, may also be appropriate. Among the interactive methods, class discussions and discussion groups are excellent means by which learners can become aware of others' values. Individualized methods tend not to be meaningful as they de-emphasize communication, a critical component of affective learning at all levels. The exception is online teaching and learning when it is primarily based on the use of discussion forums and includes links to videos, music, and the arts. Experiential methods always have the potential to increase students' awareness of values and beliefs, and usually increase interest and motivation. Field or clinical experiences, when they are relevant to the subject, are probably the most useful at the lower levels of the affective domain.

Middle Levels of the Affective Domain. At the valuing level of the affective domain, students demonstrate an acceptance of or a preference for a value. They make commitments and act, based on a new value. We need to select teaching methods that give them the opportunity to try out values, play with them, act on them, and talk about them. Instructor-centered methods are no longer as helpful. All interactive methods, especially class discussion, discussion groups, and group projects, especially when there is diversity in the group, give students a chance to engage in values-based dialogue that promotes the development of values. Among the individualized methods, independent projects can be used to increase a commitment to values, and, again, online teaching and learning that emphasizes the use of discussion forums facilitates values development. The experiential methods of field and clinical teaching, role-playing, and simulations may all provide good occasions to develop and reinforce values.

Higher Levels of the Affective Domain. At the complex organization and value levels of the affective domain, or as Hauenstein (1998) prefers, the believing and behaving levels, students formulate their own framework of values and make life decisions based on this framework. They may write a philosophy of practice, produce articles, organize demonstrations, or make career choices. Many of the requirements at this level fall outside of the domain of ordinary teaching, unless we are working with graduate students or engaging in professional development. The methods that may match what learners are doing at this stage are independent projects and field or clinical experiences.

Considering the Psychomotor Domain

Lower Levels of the Psychomotor Domain. Learning in the psychomotor domain requires a different type of involvement, namely, physical practice of the skill being taught. At the lower levels (perception and simulation), students must discriminate, recognize, distinguish by touch, follow guidelines, imitate, or try things out. The instructor-centered approach, a demonstration accompanied by a lecture, is a common and effective method. Among interactive methods, peer teaching can be useful. If some students have more experience with the skills than others, they may enjoy helping each other learn. Online teaching and learning can be used to the extent that video demonstrations of the skills to be learned are integrated into the instruction. Among the experiential methods, games and drills allow the practice and feedback necessary to begin psychomotor learning.

Middle Levels of the Psychomotor Domain. At the conformation and production levels of the psychomotor domain, skills are practiced until they conform to a standard or criteria and become habitual or routine. Students must repeatedly practice the skill and receive feedback until it becomes natural and automatic. Only experiential teaching methods work at this stage. Depending on the subject, appropriate strategies include field or clinical experiences, simulations and games, and drills.

Higher Levels of the Psychomotor Domain. When students reach the highest level of the psychomotor domain, they are able to adapt their performance to unusual circumstances or conditions, their skills become perfected, and they are able to create new ways of performing. As in the highest level of the affective domain, this level of skill may fall outside the realm of ordinary teaching unless we are, for example, coaching athletes or working with advanced craftspeople. Experiential methods—field or clinical experiences and simulations or games—are relevant approaches, as learners need to be engaged in the performance and working beyond the repetitive stage required in earlier levels.

Although there are undoubtedly creative and unusual ways we can use teaching methods that are not included in this basic matching process, I would encourage educators always to first make sure the requirement of the task as stated in the objective is provided for in the method. In Table 5-2, I summarize the appropriate methods for each domain of learning.

Considering Student Characteristics and Preferences in Selecting Methods

In Chapter Two, I describe several learner characteristics: diversity in experience, education, values, culture, and gender; multiple intelligence, emotional intelligence, and learning style; psychological type preferences, and developmental stage. Each student has a unique combination of characteristics. In practice, we can ensure that we are aware of differences among people and how student characteristics influence reactions to various teaching methods, keep the general characteristics of adult learners in mind, use a variety of methods that are appropriate to our objectives, and be flexible, provide options, and change tactics when things are not working. It will never be possible to use the ideal strategy for every person in the group. Indeed, this should not be a goal at all, for people become more versatile in the way they learn by experiencing a variety of methods. Nevertheless, we do want to work toward choosing methods that are likely to be relevant and helpful for our students.

Adult Learners' General Characteristics. Some of the general characteristics of adults as learners are discussed in Chapter Two. A great deal has been written about the methods we should use in working with adults (for example, see Brookfield, 2006 and Palmer, 2007). Most of the writing emphasizes the importance of interactive and experiential methods. I summarize some of the major points here.

Table 5-2. Matching Methods to Objectives

Instructor Centered	Interactive	Individualized	Experimental
Cognitive Domain			
Lower Levels			
• Lecture • Questioning		• Modularized	
Middle Levels			
	• Class Discussion • Discussion Groups • Group Projects	• Modularized • Online Teaching and Learning • Individual Projects	• Field or Clinical • Laboratory • Simulation and Games
Higher Levels			
	• Group Projects	• Online Teaching and Learning • Individual Projects	• Field or Clinical • Role Playing • Laboratory
Affective Domain			
Lower Levels			
• Lecture • Questioning • Demonstration	• Class Discussion • Discussion Groups	• Online Teaching and Learning	• Field or Clinical
Middle Levels			
	• Class Discussion • Discussion Groups • Group Projects	• Online Teaching and Learning • Individual Projects	• Field or Clinical • Role Playing • Simulation
Higher Levels			
		• Individual Projects	• Field or Clinical
Psychomotor Domain			
Lower Levels			
• Demonstration	• Peer Teaching	• Online Teaching and Learning	• Games • Drill
Middle Levels			
			• Field or Clinical • Simulation and Games • Drill
Higher Levels			
			• Field or Clinical • Simulation and Games

- An adult has usually chosen to attend a course or workshop and therefore has clear and specific goals. These goals must be identified and addressed through class discussion or another interactive method early in a course regardless of group size or time constraints.

- Many adults have practical goals: they hope to acquire specific skills that are relevant to their professional or personal life. Experiential methods are often the most meaningful way of working with practical goals.

- Adults come to a learning situation with a variety of experiences. It is critical to respect and use these experiences into a course or workshop, and to integrate them in a meaningful way into the content. Class discussions or discussion groups facilitate this process.

- Adults usually prefer to be self-directed. They wish to have input into their course and work on tasks relevant to their needs at their own pace. Interactive methods, such as class discussions and discussion groups, foster student input. Individualized instruction best meets their need to work on their own tasks. When this is not practical, optional activities and independent or group projects facilitate self-directed learning.

- Adults come from a variety of backgrounds and cultures and have established opinions, values, and behaviors that must be respected. Interactive methods help us to understand what those opinions, values, and behaviors are. When we want to encourage critical questioning of values and beliefs, we can use interactive methods, such as discussion groups, or experiential methods, such as role-playing and simulations.

- Although adults may have positive self-concepts in their personal lives, when they return to school, they can experience anxiety and doubt. We must provide a supportive atmosphere through discussion and group work.

Diversity in Experience, Education, Values, Culture, and Gender. Students' experiences related to a topic or objective can be considered in the selection of methods in several different ways.

- If students have no related experience and are learning something completely new, starting out with instructor-centered methods is more informative and comfortable.

- If people have practical experience in an area and are updating their knowledge or learning about the theory underlying what they already do, their experiences need to be integrated into the instruction through interactive and experiential methods.

- If learners are practicing professionals or otherwise well-versed in the subject, interactive methods in which they can share ideas and experiences are helpful.

- If students have clear ideas about what they want to learn, based on their prior experience, independent projects can meet everyone's needs.

People tend to be more comfortable with familiar teaching methods from their past educational experience. Someone who has attended lectures throughout his or her undergraduate years may feel threatened or put on the spot by discussion groups. Students who have come through instructor-centered high school programs will be disconcerted when the teacher does not take charge. Someone who has learned a trade through an experiential apprenticeship program may not know how to listen to a lecture and take notes. We need to find out something about the teaching methods our students are familiar with and then build from that base. For example, we may need to move gradually from an instructor-centered emphasis to a more interactive approach, decreasing teacher-talk time and increasing student-talk time. Or, we may need to help people learn from a lecture by providing a clear organizational framework and giving them plenty of time to ask questions. In other words, we should use the methods that are appropriate to what we are doing, but be prepared to give a little extra assistance in helping students adjust to those methods.

Learners' values, culture, and gender come into play in relation to the teaching methods they feel comfortable with and prefer. Values may be related to past educational experiences, as discussed above, but they also come from a person's cultural background. Different cultures have different expectations of the teacher's and the students' roles. Students from some cultures are not at ease with questioning or challenging a teacher or speaking out in a group. There may be differences in expectations regarding eye contact or intrusion into the physical space surrounding a person. Individuals from other cultures may be more familiar with learning through arts-based activities, images, spirituality, or symbols and metaphors. Educators who have diverse cultures represented in a group need to familiarize themselves with the values associated with those cultures. Some theorists propose that men and women tend toward different learning preferences with women being more relational and men being more autonomous (for example, see Belenky and Stanton, 2000; MacKeracher, 2004); however, educators need to be cautious in generalizing in this way and perhaps further marginalizing women as learners.

Considering Multiple Intelligences, Emotional Intelligence, Learning Style, and Psychological Type

In Chapter Two, I describe the ways in which students' learning preferences and abilities vary. As educators, it is helpful to be aware of the fundamental variations in how students learn and build this into our selection of teaching methods.

Based on a summary and simplification of the models of multiple intelligences, learning style, and psychological type, there are people who learn best when the teaching method does one of the following:

- presents analytical, focused, reflective tasks;
- encourages global thinking;
- includes physical activity;
- involves working collaboratively with others;
- provides a concrete experience;
- encourages experimentation;
- is based on competition;
- allows independent or solitary work;
- is structured and well-organized;
- supports creativity and intuition;
- involves the use of all the senses;
- fosters personal connections with the subject area.

Educators cannot do all of these things in a session, especially since it is also important to match the methods to the goals and objectives of the learning. This dilemma, arising out of research and theories that brought individual differences in learning preferences to our attention, faces all teachers and has no easy solution.

Providing as much variety as possible, without abandoning the match between methods and objectives, is probably the most commonly suggested way of coping with learning preferences and is a good general rule of thumb. With experience and sensitive awareness of the differences among students, educators become increasingly adept at modifying what they are doing and changing methods when it becomes apparent a particular strategy is grating against the learning style of some or most of the group. The key is awareness. A good understanding of individual differences and knowing that others do not necessarily learn in the same way that the educator does help him or her find a way to relate to different styles.

It is also well to remember that most learner preferences are not innate or static. People learn to learn in different ways with experience (Kolb, 1984, makes this point very well). Teaching in a way that directly corresponds with students' styles may be doing students a disservice by removing the opportunity to experience other styles.

Considering Developmental Stage As stated in Chapter Two, developmental stage theory recognizes that people tend to move from a simple authority-based ways of knowing to an integrated or more complex understanding of the world. To select teaching methods with this in mind, two considerations stand out. One is to make sure that we are not teaching in a way that is out of synch with where most of the students are developmentally. The second is to foster the transition from simple to complex stages. King and Kitchener (1994, pp. 230-234) list sound strategies for use at each of their stages, some examples of which follow.

- If students are at the level of reasoning (stage 2) where knowledge is seen to be certain and authorities have the answers, we should use methods that encourage them to consider two different interpretations of the same poem, event, or study, provide arguments on two sides of an issue, or identify evidence for different opinions on the same issue. A lecture followed by discussion is an appropriate vehicle for doing this.

- Students at the stage where knowledge is seen to be certain in some areas, but uncertain in others (stage 3) need opportunities to evaluate inadequate arguments, come up with alternative perspectives on an issue, and critique points of view. Discussion groups (face-to-face or online) provide such opportunities.

- When students reach the point where they see knowledge as uncertain because of the limitations of the person (stage 4), they need to compare good and bad arguments, evaluate arguments, and see how authors arrive at conclusions. Discussion groups (face-to-face or online), group projects, and independent projects can accomplish these kinds of objectives.

- For students who have reached the stage in their reasoning where they recognize that interpretation is inherent in all understanding and no knowledge is certain (stage 5), King and Kitchener suggest learning activities such as comparing and contrasting competing points of view, identifying evidence and arguments for points of view and determining which has the stronger support, and analyzing controversial issues. Group projects and independent projects are good methods to use at this stage.

- When students see knowledge as uncertain and understood only in relationship to context and evidence (stage 6), sample assignments include developing and defending arguments for a particular point of view and providing one's own organization of a given field of study. Independent projects allow for such learning.

As students move to higher levels of reasoning, the teaching methods allow for increased autonomy and independent work. At the highest level (stage 6), students may be writing a thesis or engaging in a research project.

Considering Teacher Preferences in Selecting Methods I have always been concerned that the implication underlying much of the literature on teaching is that we, as educators, can use all methods equally effectively. Just as students have different styles, personalities, and preferences, so do teachers. It is unlikely that any one person can display all the characteristics of good teachers included in the literature. We are supposed to be dynamic lecturers, good listeners, creative, well organized, flexible, structured, caring, up-to-date, practical, empathic, supportive, challenging, and innovative.

Elsewhere, I encourage educators to develop a personal teaching style and select and adapt methods based on their values, preferences, and styles (Cranton, 2001). This is not to say that a superb practitioner in one style cannot be equally proficient in another. For example, a good lecturer may also facilitate outstanding role-plays. But as people, educators have likes and dislikes, preferences and aversions, and strengths and weaknesses. It is best to acknowledge these, work with them, be authentic, and then also work to develop and grow. The following short case studies illustrate this process.

> Paula is an introverted person. She is well organized, logical, and analytical in her teaching and learning style. She enjoys her subject, finance and accounting, but hates to lecture. In some ways, instructor-centered methods suit Paula and match the requirements of her objectives, but her introversion makes her uncomfortable standing in front of a group and speaking. Paula could set a personal goal to develop her lecturing, demonstration, and questioning skills. In her classes she could assign structured group projects in which students work on well-defined tasks, and intersperse these group projects with short lectures or summaries of points that arise during the group work. In this way she can remain true to her nature, while, at the same time, continuing to develop new skills.

> Tony loves people. He is enthusiastic, caring, and innovative. He teaches English as a second language to freshman university students. He may be somewhat disorganized, but his charisma makes up for the mistakes he makes in outlining topics in his teaching. Tony works best with interactive methods, and they also suit his subject. At the same time, Tony could work to develop his organizational skills by spending more time on his course outlines, asking colleagues for comments, and experimenting with various learning sequences.

> Peter is an intuitive person. His goal as a teacher is to change the lives of his students. He is full of energy and enthusiasm. Peter is also well organized and able to manage a heavy

workload with a minimum of fuss. Peter teaches forestry students who are there to learn practical skills they will use on the job. They do not see that their lives need to be changed. Peter selects experiential methods, given his subject, but he needs to find a way to let his intuition and future-oriented nature shine through. Peter does this by taking on the responsibility of working with industry to reform the programs in his college. He sets a goal to better understand his students' practical needs and decides to do a small research project on this.

Andrea is a down-to-earth, practical person who enjoys working to solve problems in the real lives of people. She works for a social service agency where she is responsible for the professional development of caseworkers. Many of her students are interested in reforming the system to deal with their very heavy caseloads. Andrea likes to use interactive methods, but she prefers to focus on working with clients rather than systemic issues. She could incorporate independent projects into the methods she uses, encouraging students to explore their interests in reform. In group sessions, she could then encourage students to relate their client cases to their reform work. Andrea would give herself the opportunity to learn different perspectives while she remained authentic and true to her own nature.

Considering Context in Selecting Methods

Sometimes characteristics of the instructional situation or the context in which we work need to be considered in our selection of methods. These may include:

- the size of the group;
- whether or not the instruction is required or participation is voluntary;
- the physical facilities;
- the resources;
- the time of day of the class or session.

Group size usually only directly affects the choice of teaching methods when the class is quite large. With more than about 30 people in a group, whole-class discussions begin to lose their effectiveness. It is simply too hard for everyone to participate. Large classes hamper nearly all experiential learning methods as well, and individualized learning is problematic in relation to management and record keeping. Usually, large groups occur only at the introductory levels in higher education or in one-time presentations, such as professional development days. In these cases, instructor-centered methods are probably most appropriate. Occasionally independent learning can take place, particularly if assistance is available for tutoring and feedback.

Even if the group is large, educators should not give up on interactive methods, though, if the objectives require them. For example, with a group of 120 college teachers registered in a professional development session on the evaluation of teaching, what can be done? Most people in the group likely have had several years of teaching experience. A lecture would be inappropriate both for the topic and for the people in the audience, all of whom have experience with evaluation and probably have opinions on how it should or should not be done. First, prior to the session, the room could be arranged so that people are sitting in 12 groups of 10 individuals each. After an introductory ice-breaking activity during which people get to know the others at their table, there could be a short overview of the topic, using a lecture format. From there, the topic could be broken into its various components, such as purposes of evaluation, aspects of teaching that can be evaluated, sources of information to use, instruments and methods, how to develop and apply criteria, and using the results. For each aspect, an activity could be used to foster group discussion. With all people already in groups, there would be no shuffling of tables and chairs. The 12 groups would go through each of the exercises; after each, one group (or two, depending on time) would summarize the main points in their discussion for the large group. The teacher would introduce and summarize each activity. In this way an interactive method—group discussion—can be used in a way that is focused, structured, and carefully timed so as to be manageable. While more difficult, this approach is probably more effective than an instructor-centered lecture. People are busy, talking to each other, thinking about the topic, using their experiences, and relating new ideas to what they already know.

Whether the learning experience is *required or voluntary* is likely to affect learner interest and motivation, which in turn influences the selection of methods. People who have been ordered to attend a training session may be trying to just get through the day; on the other hand, those who have chosen a course or workshop have their own personal or professional goals related to the content and therefore are ready to pursue an independent project or get involved in discussion groups. Sometimes, even when instruction is imposed, people do have high extrinsic motivation—they want to keep their job or get a promotion. In this case, they may express more interest in receiving efficient communication of material by an expert. It is important to find out why the students are there and consider this in the selection of methods.

When students are required to attend a course or workshop, the educator needs to work hard to get them involved and interested. Learning needs to be enjoyable and be so immediately—in the first half-hour of the workshop or the first class of a course. So even if the objectives indicate that lectures should be used to introduce basic concepts, this can be put off initially in favor of group work, games, or simulations in order to get the group interested and involved.

The *physical facilities* of the room or institution can influence the choice of teaching methods. If, for example, there are few facilities for independent research, such as a good library or a quiet working environment, independent learning methods are harder to use. If the room lacks any moveable chairs and tables, it is more difficult to organize group discussions. Whenever it is possible, an inspection of the physical facilities in advance of the session or course can be helpful.

Other institutional *resources* may also affect our choice of methods. For example, there may be limited access to smart classrooms, so that the incorporation of internet sites or social networking sites could be restricted.

Sometimes, at what *time of day* the instruction is offered may be a consideration in the selection of methods and materials. In an evening or late afternoon session, especially if people are arriving after a day of work, the methods need to allow for changes of pace, variety, interaction, active involvement, humor, and drama. Tired people listening to a lecture in the evening tend not to learn very much. Most people have preferred times of day, times when we feel most mentally alert. If students are at a low point because of an 8:00 a.m. class, one right after lunch, or an evening session, the teaching methods need to make learning interesting and fun. Interactive methods and field experiences help people out of a downtime in their cycle.

For full-time students in colleges and universities, the nature of the class immediately preceding or following the session may also be a consideration in planning activities. Learners who have arrived in a required history class after leaving their favorite physical education course face an abrupt change in environment. The choice of the first method used in the class can smooth the transition from one subject to another.

Summary

Teaching methods vary in the extent to which they encourage self-direction, how interactive they are, or the level of reasoning or critical thinking required. I choose to categorize them in a way that facilitates matching methods to objectives. I am most interested, here, in the nature of learning required by the objective and how we can use methods that best engage students in the process and facilitate that learning

Instructor-centered methods, such as lectures, questioning, and demonstration, are those in which the direction of the communication is primarily from the teacher to the students. Underlying these methods is the assumption is that the teacher has information to convey or give to the students. Students acquire concepts, facts, and the fundamentals of the subject.

The interactive methods of class discussion, discussion groups (including online discussion forums), group projects, and peer teaching are those in which communication takes place between students and teacher, and among students. Here, it is assumed that knowledge is constructed through dialogue among people. Students bring their ideas, experiences, values, beliefs and opinions, and by working with others, create knowledge that they would not attain by working on their own, listening to a person talk, or reading a book.

Individualized learning methods—modularized instruction, online teaching and learning, and independent projects—are those in which students work primarily on their own and at their own pace. The assumption is that people can use resources and engage in research and investigation to acquire basic information, discover new concepts and ideas, solve problems, critique theories, and synthesize information from a variety of sources.

Experiential learning methods, including field or clinical experiences, laboratory work, role-playing, simulations and games, and drills, require students to take action in either a real or a simulated setting. Underlying the selection of experiential learning methods is the assumption that the objectives require students actually to operate equipment, acquire physical skills, practice, or experience a situation.

In matching methods to objectives, we need to consider the requirements of the task that are implicit or explicit in the objective. If students are expected to describe or define something, they must be given the opportunity to describe or define. If they are expected to synthesize ideas, they need to actually synthesize ideas.

Although matching methods to the nature of learning outlined in the objectives is the first priority, learner characteristics and preferences need to be considered as well. The general characteristics of adult learners, the experience and background of a specific group, our students' learning and personality preferences, and their developmental stage all may play some part in our selection of teaching methods. Teacher preferences and styles can also be considered.

Finally, there are times when such factors as the size of the group, whether attendance is required, the physical facilities, or even the time of day of a session influence our choice of methods.

Chapter 6

Selecting Materials

Materials are essential for learning, even if the "materials" are spoken words. Certain materials often naturally accompany the methods we use: PowerPoint slides may accompany a lecture, models may be displayed in a demonstration, readings may precede a discussion, electronic articles are used in online learning, and real objects may provide the foundation for experiential learning methods.

Materials do more than simply deliver information. Good materials have the potential to help students become more independent, and facilitate interaction around a common theme. Materials can present a clear explanation of complex relations, an overview of unfamiliar topics, or a checklist for review. Materials also help learners visualize. Sometimes, class materials can provide memorable and vivid examples to illuminate content through film, internet clips, music, and poetry.

In this chapter, I first discuss three components of materials: delivery system, message, and form. I then describe several types of materials and consider each in relation to the method or methods commonly associated with them, who controls the pacing, the optimal group size for their use, and the degree to which students can interact with the material. Third, I examine how we should select materials, based on the nature of the expected learning. Fourth, I review some student characteristics that can influence our selection of materials. Finally, I consider materials selection in relation to the teaching and learning context.

Three Components of Materials

All instructional materials communicate a message to students using some kind of delivery system, such as a book, a software package, or a lab specimen slide. Materials have a form that varies from concrete to abstract: for example the words on the pages of a book are abstract compared to the actual bacteria on the specimen slide. Although I discuss each of these components separately for purposes of clarification, in reality they are inseparable.

Delivery system The delivery system of teaching materials includes such things as print on paper, PowerPoint slides, electronic readings, computers, and DVDs. The delivery system includes both the physical form of the materials and the hardware or equipment used to present it. For PowerPoint slides, the slide is the physical form of the material and computer is the hardware. The paper and ink in a textbook constitute the physical form of the reading material; there is no equipment or hardware involved. A person delivers spoken words as a material; the teacher is technically the delivery system. Knowing what the delivery system is tells us nothing about the message: a DVD might contain an interview with Carl Jung, classical music, or an exposition on the four food groups.

Message The information communicated using a delivery system is called the message. The same message can be communicated in a variety of ways—through spoken words, books, films, or by examining real objects—though not all messages can be communicated using all delivery systems. The combination of message and delivery needs to be matched to the nature of the learning, as well as the teaching method.

Form The form of the message is often the most important consideration when selecting or developing instructional materials. Message form can be placed along a continuum from concrete (real things) to abstract (symbols). To study the bones of the human skeleton, an actual skeleton is the example of the most concrete form of materials. The *real thing* is three-dimensional and has the advantage of displaying actual characteristics, such as size, color, texture, weight, structure, and flexibility. Real objects stimulate additional senses. They can provide olfactory (smell), gustatory (taste), and tactile (touch) stimuli, as well as visual and auditory stimuli. When a real skeleton is displayed, students can see and feel the bones. They can also hear the sounds made by bone moving against bone at the joints.

If a real skeleton is not available, the next most concrete representation is a *model* of the skeleton. A model is still three-dimensional and can be the actual human size. As real objects do, models allow for perception of dimensionality. Students can move their heads, physically move around it, or manipulate the model in order to view it from various angles. Models can provide olfactory, gustatory, tactile, auditory, and visual stimuli, but some of the stimuli may not be realistic—the feel, smell, or taste may be unnatural. A model is a replica or imitation and therefore has lost some of the actual characteristics of real bones. The weight, texture, or structure may be different. The color may be off, and the plastic bones may be less brittle than real bones. We might tell students, "A real bone, when cut in half would reveal an ossified structure," but students cannot see the ossified structure. They need to imagine it, to understand ossification on an abstract level. Some realism is lost.

If a model of a skeleton is not available, the next most concrete form of material would be photographs. Now many characteristics of the real thing are absent. Students cannot touch the bones to feel the weight or texture. Photographs are not likely to be the actual size, and the color may not be realistic. There are two rather than three dimensions. Photographs are illusions or representations of the real thing. The form of the message has become less realistic and more abstract. More abstract still are drawings of a skeleton. In a drawing, some details may be left out and others highlighted. A full-color drawing with natural shading and perspective is more concrete than a line drawing, but both are illusions—they only resemble the real thing.

Several forms of moving illusions, such as films, can provide partial appreciation of dimensionality. Although students cannot manipulate or move around flat, two-dimensional visual images, the camera can act as our head and body by showing an object from several angles and distances. We are given the illusion of three dimensions. Computer graphics can produce rotating two-dimensional images, creating a 3-D effect. Virtual reality techniques further enhance the feeling of three dimensions in a two-dimensional medium. Students are offered angles and views impossible to detect in the real world. The structure of a molecule, for example, can be shown in various scales and perspectives that could not be seen with the human eye.

At the most abstract level of the continuum, students can read about the bones of the skeleton. Words are symbols representing objects or ideas. They bear no physical resemblance to the real thing so that students are required to visualize the real thing from the words they read. Symbols are the most common form of material that we use in education.

In Table 6-1, the example of the skeleton is depicted along the concrete-abstract continuum. Real things are actual objects, imitations are three-dimensional models, illusions are two-dimensional representations, and symbols are abstract referents, either visual as in written material or auditory as in spoken words.

Table 6-1. Forms of Instructional Materials: The Concrete —— Abstract Continuum				
	CONCRETE ◄		►	ABSTRACT
Forms	**Real Things**	**Imitations**	**Illusions**	**Symbols**
Examples	• actual skeleton	• plastic model of skeleton	• photograph or drawing	• words describing skeleton

Description of Materials

In this section, I describe how certain materials are commonly associated with certain teaching methods, which person controls the pacing when the material is used, the size of the group with which the material can be used, and the degree of responsiveness of the material.

The *associated method* is the instructional technique that most often incorporates certain materials. Materials are used with one of the categories of instructional methods I describe in Chapter Five: instructor-centered, interactive, individualized, and experiential.

Pacing refers to the rate at which information is presented to the students. The pace can be controlled by the teacher, as it is when she is giving a lecture, by the learner, as it is when he is reading a textbook, or by the producer, the person who creates a film or DVD.

Group size refers to the optimal size of the group with which the material should be used. Many materials are quite flexible; DVDs for example, can be viewed by an individual at his or her personal computer or projected onto a large screen for a group of almost any size. or shown to a large group.

By *responsiveness* I mean the degree to which the material changes in response to what the student may do. If we imagine a student alone in a room with only the material, the potential of the material to be responsive becomes clearer. For example if someone is in a room with a chalkboard on which an outline has been written, and that person does not understand the outline, the chalkboard will not say anything to explain itself. Neither will it change itself when one student leaves the room and another enters. Similarly, with practice questions and feedback included in a text, there is no responsive or variable interaction — the questions in the book do not change depending on the student's reaction.

Spoken Words The spoken word is probably the most commonly used instructional material. Speech is the basis of the lecture method and also plays a part in all other methods. Demonstrations and all experiential methods are usually accompanied by spoken words. Interactive methods are often debriefed or summarized by an oral presentation. In discussions, students' spoken words are a form of material. The teacher controls the pacing, except when speech is used in conjunction with interactive methods. The associated method determines the optimal group size for the spoken word: with lectures, this material works well for large groups, with demonstrations, for smaller groups. The spoken word is a responsive material, since the person who delivers it can change what is being presented in reaction to students' questions, comments, and interests.

The advantages of the spoken word as a material are clear. No equipment is required, words are inexpensive and easy to formulate. We just talk to our students. The main disadvantage is that spoken words are transient. They are gone after they are spoken. Students need to remember what is said and know how to take notes. On the other hand, the spoken word can easily be accompanied by written summaries or outlines on paper or PowerPoint slides. Lecture notes can be uploaded onto a common platform to which students all have access.

Chalkboard or White Board The chalkboard or white board is a very commonly used instructional material. In preparation for class, on the chalkboard we can provide a plan for the day's proceedings or present a drawing, set of formulae, or definitions that will remain visible throughout the session. When used in this way, the material acts as an organizer for students. Even if the accompanying oral presentation is teacher-paced, students can use the board as a reference as needed. Chalkboards or white boards are also often used during a presentation. We can create a drawing to illustrate a point while we are talking, or jot down main points or unfamiliar words. While the teacher paces the material, students have some control as well, by using the board for a visual review of information. Chalkboards work well with groups of up to 30 people, but beyond that are too difficult for everyone to see. Like lectures, this material is responsive since what is written on the chalkboard can be added to or changed any time according to student reaction.

Using a chalkboard or white board requires no technical expertise, except clear handwriting, and is both convenient and inexpensive. Writing on a board means that the educator turns away from the students temporarily, but this can create time to stop and reflect or review.

Text Instructors nearly always rely on texts and other printed or electronic materials as instructional materials. Texts can accompany any teaching method. They are self-pacing materials usually used by individuals, although electronic text can be projected to a group for joint reading (in this case, we lose the advantage of students reading at their own pace). Texts are not responsive—they do not change based on students' reactions.

The greatest advantage of texts as materials is that students can read on their own at their own pace. They can also reread and review text materials and easily access whatever portion of text they wish in whatever order they choose. It is important to make sure that the printed or electronic materials are written at the appropriate reading level for the students, and are interesting and relevant. The reading should be a part of the teaching method, not an aside. Discussions should be based on the reading, and lectures should elaborate on points in the reading. It is frustrating for students when readings are assigned but not integrated into the course.

Specimens and models Specimens and models serve a similar purpose and are treated together here. Specimens are real things, such as microscopic creatures used in zoology, a camera used in a photography workshop, a patient on whom a student nurse practices or applies skills, or a real plane flown by a trainee pilot. Models are imitations of the real thing, such as a plastic representation of a DNA structure used in biology, a cut-away replica of a fuel injection system for auto mechanics, or life-like mannequins used in cardio-pulmonary resuscitation training. Both specimens and models offer direct experience to the learner. Real objects have certain advantages; however, in some cases, imitations are more appropriate as they can offer a unique view (e.g., a cross-section of the earth's crust) or a controlled experience (e.g., CPR practice on a simulated victim, or pilot training in flight simulators).

Specimens and models can be associated with almost any method, but are most commonly used with instructor-centered and experiential methods. In a lecture, an actual object can serve as an example. Demonstrations, usually both directed and paced by the teacher, are carried out with specimens or models so that students can see the procedures or sequence of activities. By definition, experiential learning always requires students to work with specimens or models. In simulations, the pacing may be determined by either the teacher or the learner. Flight simulators and resuscitation models, for example, create a realistic, non-threatening experience for the learner. In both of these examples, speed and accuracy are crucial so the presenter (the simulator) controls the pace. If students respond too slowly, they could lose the patient or the plane. In other types of simulations where timing is unimportant, the learner can set the pace. For example, in individualized methods, models and specimens may accompany modules or be a part of independent study. Students can, at their own pace, observe or work with the materials, perhaps following study guides, directions, or questions in a text.

Specimens and models are most effectively used with individuals or with smaller groups where everyone can have the opportunity to see and touch the material.

Specimens and models vary in their potential to respond to students. Inanimate objects tend not to be responsive, but computer-based simulators offer opportunity for realistic interactions. Animate specimens, such as microscopic planaria or actors playing the part of patients, provide a full range of realistic interaction.

Both specimens and models can be expensive to create, buy, hire, or use. Yet, the direct concrete experience provided makes them a worthwhile investment especially when the objectives require that students be able to see, touch, and manipulate things.

PowerPoint Slides A PowerPoint slide is created on a computer using PowerPoint software and projected onto a large screen for student viewing. It may contain words, numbers, charts, graphs, or drawings.

PowerPoint slides are most often used as part of teacher-paced lectures. Sometimes they function in much the same way as a chalkboard, showing an outline or agenda for a session, reinforcing main points, or showing the relationships among concepts. Good slides, prepared in color and including drawings or photographs, can provide an interesting focal point during an instructor-centered session. With interactive methods such as group projects, groups can use slides to summarize their work for presentation back to the larger group.

PowerPoint slides differ from the chalkboard or white board in some noticeable ways. The image is projected and therefore can be made quite large for use with bigger groups. There are no space limitations since any number of slides can be prepared in advance and used one at a time. But perhaps most importantly, the slides allow for a much more attractive and interesting presentation than does a chalkboard. They may be accompanied by music, and there can be, to a limited extent, some animation.

PowerPoint slides can be misused: the most common mistake is to include too much information on a single slide. Also the format of the software with its headings and bullet points tends to determine the structure of the information presented in ways that may not be appropriate.

Compact discs   Compact discs, or CDs, on which sound has been recorded, can be used to bring music, interviews, or speeches into the classroom. As part of an instructor-centered method, a CD can provide variety or bring the voice of an expert to the group. As part of interactive methods, listening to an interview or speech can form the basis for discussion or group work. CDs are also used in individualized instruction.

The producer of the CD determines the pace. The content itself is not responsive, that is, does not change in response to audience reaction, but the CD can be stopped, replayed, and advanced, giving some degree of control to the user.

CDs are easy to use. They are small, mobile, inexpensive, and reusable. They bring otherwise inaccessible people and experiences into the classroom. Students can review the material, take CDs home, or play them in the car. On the other hand, as CDs provide only verbal information, they should not be used when visualization of an experience is a part of the objective.

Photographs   The term photograph here refers to pictures printed on paper or saved electronically on a computer. Photographs can range in size from a small snapshot to a wall-size print. Digital photographs can be projected onto a large screen. Photographs can be used as part of an instructor-paced lecture. They can be shown temporarily when we want to illustrate by example or be left on display throughout a presentation. With interactive methods, photographs can be handed around from one person to another as a focal point of discussion or brought in by group members to illustrate personal points of view. In individualized learning methods, photographs often accompany a text or study guide and may be accompanied by questions. In online teaching and learning, digital photographs can be made available on the course site. Photographs can be studied at length, with the learner selecting the pace and the focus.

Photographs can bring inaccessible visual experiences, such as an underwater scene or mountaintop view, into the classroom. Thousands of images are available on the Internet. Photographs can also easily be taken using a digital camera and uploaded to a common site for learners to view.

Film A film is projected on a screen allowing viewing by any size of group. Films are now almost always digitized and available on DVDs. A film includes motion and sound. Not only can realistic motion be captured, but also slow-motion and time-lapse techniques allow viewers to see things that are imperceptible to the human eye, such as the speeded-up growth of a plant (time lapse) or the contractions of each muscle in a dancer's leg (slow motion). Films are often used in conjunction with instructor-centered methods to bring the outside world into the classroom. The producer determines the visual and audio sequence and the tone and pace of information presentation; however the film can be stopped for discussion and questions at any point.

Films are excellent for providing the basis for discussion in interactive methods. In individualized learning methods, students may view films as a part of their studies.

Table 6-2 Summary of Instructional Materials

Material	Associated Methods	Group Size	Pacing	Responsive
Spoken Words				
	• Instructor-centered • Interactive • Individualized • Experiential	• Any • Small to Medium • Small • Small	• Teacher • Teacher or Learner • Learner • Teacher or Learner	• Yes • Yes • Yes • Yes
Chalkboard or Whiteboard				
	• Instructor-centered • Interactive	• Medium • Small to Medium	• Teacher or Learner • Teacher or Learner	• No • No
Text				
	• Instructor-centered • Interactive • Individualized • Experiential	• Any • Small to Medium • Small • Small	• Learner • Learner • Learner • Learner	• No • No • No • No
Specimen				
	• Instructor-centered • Interactive • Individualized • Experiential	• Medium • Small to Medium • Small • Small	• Teacher • Teacher • Learner • Learner	• Yes, if animate • Yes, if animate • Yes, if animate • Yes, if animate
Model				
	• Instructor-centered • Interactive • Individualized • Experiential	• Medium • Small to Medium • Small • Small	• Teacher • Teacher • Learner • Learner	• Variable • Variable • Variable • Variable
PowerPoint Slides				
	• Instructor-centered • Interactive	• Any • Any	• Teacher • Learner	• No • No
CDs				
	• Instructor-centered • Interactive • Individualized	• Any • Any • Any	• Producer • Producer or Learner • Producer or Learner	• No • No • No
Photographs				
	• Instructor-centered • Interactive • Individualized	• Any • Any • Any	• Teacher • Teacher or Learner • Learner	• No • No • No
Film or DVD				
	• Instructor-centered • Interactive • Individualized	• Any • Any • Any	• Producer • Producer • Producer	• No • No • No

Matching Materials to Objectives

In Chapter Five, I describe how the nature of the expected learning or the requirements of the task as stated in the objective leads us to an appropriate teaching method. Students need to have the opportunity to do what the objective indicates they will learn to do. Similarly, the materials we choose must complement the method and allow the students to have appropriate experiences. If students are learning to repair a saw, an experiential teaching method is necessary, and the material must include a real saw. Reading about the repair process may be helpful after students have worked with the real thing, but few people can learn to repair a saw using written materials alone. Similarly, if students are learning to think critically, they need to work with symbols, with written texts presenting a variety of viewpoints and arguments. Just as certain methods were more appropriate with each different level of learning in each of the cognitive, affective, and psychomotor domains, so certain materials are more effective. These are explored below.

Lower Levels of the Cognitive Domain At the knowledge and comprehension levels of the cognitive domain, students are learning to define, identify, illustrate, and remember. Instructor-centered and individualized methods are used. Students are required to work with words, either spoken or written in order to define, label, conceptualize, or identify. Chalkboards or white boards and PowerPoint slides may be helpful delivery systems for conveying written and oral materials. Computerized materials can enhance learning by simultaneously presenting text and graphics. In some subjects, drawings and photographs, models, or real things are needed in order to associate words with objects. Students learning anatomy read a text, study drawings, and do dissections.

Middle Levels of the Cognitive Domain At the application and analysis levels, students are learning to solve, apply, and relate ideas, and analyze concepts. Interactive, individualized, and experiential methods are all appropriate, depending on the discipline. The requirement of the task in application and analysis is to work with ideas and concepts—read and talk about them with others. Spoken and written words form the foundation of this kind of learning.

Chalkboards and PowerPoint slides can be used to illustrate problem solving; discussions on CD or in films and DVDs can help students analyze different points of view. Students analyzing the fall of Communism could read about the sequence of events, listen to interviews with Communist party and opposition members, or watch a film on the former East Germany. When students research this topic on the Internet, downloaded material can also help meet the requirements of the task.

Higher Levels of the Cognitive Domain At the synthesis and evaluation level, students produce, design, create, write, and evaluate. Group and individual projects are the methods most commonly associated with this type of learning. Students work primarily with written words in text format, though they may also demonstrate their learning through an oral presentation, the production of an CD or DVD, or the design of a model. Discussion and therefore the use of spoken words also play an important role. Students who plan to conduct a review and synthesis of the literature on Jungian psychology would read extensively and perhaps discuss their ideas with the instructor and their peers. They might prepare a presentation of their findings as a part of their learning.

Lower Levels of the Affective Domain At the receiving and responding levels of the affective domain, students are exposed to beliefs, values, and opinions. The requirements of the task include attending, listening, showing interest, and expressing enjoyment. Instructor-centered, interactive, and experiential methods can all be appropriate. A wide variety of materials can be used to exhibit values: spoken words, text, photographs, PowerPoint slides, films, and computerized materials. Students learning about substance abuse may read articles, watch a film, and investigate materials on the Internet. When experiential methods are used, real people and situations may model or demonstrate a value. Students can visit a rehabilitation center and perhaps meet with a counselor.

Middle Levels of the Affective Domain At the valuing level, students make a commitment and act on a new value. They need to talk and read about values, and see them in action. Interactive and experiential methods are most likely to provide the environment in which this can occur. Spoken words, texts, and films all have the potential to foster students' commitment to values. Nursing students who are making a commitment to caring for patients regardless of their culture and background can learn from, for example, discussion, reading, or seeing films of people with diverse backgrounds in a health care setting. Experiences in field and clinical settings can be a powerful way of reinforcing a value or providing an opportunity to act on it.

Higher Levels of the Affective Domain   At the higher levels of the affective domain—organization and value complex, or believing and behaving—students make life decisions based on their framework of values. Independent projects and experiential methods facilitate this process. Although almost any form of material can play a part in the learning, written and spoken words or contact with real people and situations are more likely at this stage. A student who decides to pursue a career in counseling, for example, will have read extensively, discussed the decision with many people, and interacted with clients and practicing counselors.

Lower Levels of the Psychomotor Domain   At the perception and simulation levels of the psychomotor domain, students are required to discriminate, distinguish by touch, follow guidelines, try things out, and imitate behaviors. Instructor-centered methods are most commonly used. The materials needed depend on the subject. Generally, though, an explanation in the form of written text or spoken words and a real person or a model demonstrating the performance is necessary. In addition, demonstrations can be conveyed through photographs or films. A student learning to operate an X-ray machine may listen to the instructor's explanation, examine the machine herself, and begin to experiment with its use.

Middle Levels of the Psychomotor Domain   At the conformation and production levels, skills are practiced until they become habitual. Experiential learning methods are required—there is no other way to learn this except by doing it. Students need to work with models or real things. A student learning to administer an IV must practice doing so with a real needle and either a real patient or a realistic model.

Table 6-3. Matching Materials to Objectives

Type of Objective	Requirements of the Task	Type of Material
Lower level, cognitive	• Define • Label • Identity • Conceptualize • Remember	• Spoken words • Text • Chalkboard or Whiteboard • PowerPoint slides • Computerized materials • Photographs • Models • Real things
Middle level, cognitive	• Apply • Problem solve • Analyze	• Spoken words • Text • Chalkboard or Whiteboard • PowerPoint slides • Film/DVD • Computerized materials
Upper level, cognitive	• Produce • Design • Create • Write • Evaluate	• Spoken words • Text • Models • Computerized materials
Lower level, affective	• Attend • Listen • Show interest • Enjoy	• Spoken words • Text • Photographs • Film/DVD • Computerized materials • Real things
Middle level, affective	• Value • Make commitments	• Spoken words • Text • Film • Real things
Upper level, affective	• Choose • Make life decisions	• Spoken words • Text • Real things
Lower level, psychomotor	• Discriminate • Follow guidelines • Imitate	• Spoken words • Text • Specimens • Models • Photographs • Film/DVD
Middle level, psychomotor	• Practice	• Specimens • Models
Upper level, psychomotor	• Perfect performance • Create novel performance	• Specimens • Models

Higher Levels of the Psychomotor Domain   At the mastery level, skills are perfected and students are able to adapt to unusual circumstances or create novel ways of performing. Only experiential methods are relevant. As with the middle levels in the psychomotor domain, students must carry out the performance. Real things and, less frequently, models are the only materials we can use, although using digital film may be useful for feedback. Students creating their own modern dance routine work with other dancers, their own bodies, and perhaps costumes or other props.

Considering Student Characteristics and Preferences in Selecting Materials

While considering how to take into account student characteristics in materials selection, I was reminded of an excerpt from an interview Susan Wilcox (1995) conducted with George Geis, an expert instructional designer.

> Instructional designers have to be more sophisticated about their clients. We did two studies. We were looking at various micro techniques for teaching psychomotor skills and the material we chose was the Russian alphabet because most people don't know the Russian alphabet. We had a forward program and a backward program. Very elaborate stuff. We'd spent months designing it. People did variations... And they'd do OK. One of our students in the beginning said, "Can I look at the alphabet?" We said, "Well, you're not supposed to," and he said, "What if I just looked at it?" It was the end of a long day, and we said OK. He took it and copied it and within half an hour he could write the whole alphabet. (George Geis speaking in an interview, May 10, 1995.)

The first priority in materials selection is to ensure that the material both complements the teaching method and matches the requirements of the task as was specified in the learning objectives. However, people react to materials in different ways. Ideally, we consider student characteristics in our selection of methods. Similarly, we need to attend to student styles, preferences, prior experience or knowledge, and cultural background in choosing appropriate materials. Just as it is not possible to meet all individual needs at any one time with our choice of methods (as was noted in Chapter Five), it is not possible to do so with materials. However, it is easier to offer options and alternatives in materials than with methods, since many materials are used outside of the classroom and even within the classroom, there can be optional materials. Some students can read a text, others can watch a video and share what they learned. While providing a variety of materials is essential, it is equally important to encourage students to work with unfamiliar or less-preferred materials so they expand their repertoire of styles and preferences.

Beyond this general guideline, there are a few things that we should consider more carefully.

- Some people learn more easily by listening and others by seeing. It is always a good idea both to say something and to present it in writing. For example, objectives for a session or guidelines for a discussion group can be stated orally and also displayed on a PowerPoint slide or distributed as a handout.

- When we are using real things or models as materials, it is helpful to remember that some students have a well-developed spatial intelligence (Gardner's multiple intelligences; see Chapter Two), and others do not. The student who is all-thumbs will benefit from having clear written materials and drawings to follow as she or he learns to work with concrete objects.

- When students have considerable prior experience with a concept, using symbolic forms of instruction is appropriate. Students can manipulate related ideas and work on an abstract level. However, when students have little or no experience with a concept, working at a concrete level will be more successful. Concrete materials, such as real things and models, allow people to experience the full range of attributes associated with an object, process, or procedure.

- When we begin with concrete materials, we should follow this introduction with materials that require the manipulation of symbols to facilitate the development of students' ability to work with symbols.

- If the group includes learners who have special language, visual, auditory, or physical needs, these must be taken into consideration. Reading materials, for example, must be selected with care when people are learning in their second language. Using materials in more than one form, say symbols and illusions, is helpful.

- People from different cultural backgrounds may have varying experiences with materials, and some may prefer arts-based materials, images and symbols over text-based materials (or in addition to text-based materials).

Considering Context in Selecting Materials

The context within which educators are teaching may influence the choice of materials. For instance, a limited photocopying budget restricts the use of print materials and likely increases a reliance on electronic copies and online materials. The size of the group sometimes has a bearing on our choices. Fifty students gathered around a model of an engine benefit less than a group, each of whom has a photograph or drawing, even though the model may better suit the requirements of the learning task. Teachers learn to work around and adapt to these kinds of constraints. At the same time, it is important to speak up when the context interferes with offering good quality teaching and learning experiences.

Although many contextual variables that influence the selection of materials are specific to institutions or programs, some general guidelines may be helpful.

- Educators should move along the concrete to abstract continuum in the choice of materials. For example, if using the real thing is too expensive or impractical, a model can be used. If a model is not available or is too expensive, a photograph or several photographs from different perspectives can be a substitute. However, some of the qualities of the real thing are lost when moving toward more abstract materials.

- The chalkboard or white board provides an inexpensive alternative to photocopied materials. Posting notes on a course site is also helpful, but it is less spontaneous.

- Videos can be downloaded from the internet or borrowed from the library (on DVD).

- Students can work in pairs or even in threes on computers to access computerized materials should computer facilities not allow everyone to have private access.

- Teachers can bring their laptop to class to play DVDs or CDs or show PowerPoint slides. Students, too, are often happy to bring their personal equipment, including laptop computers, to class.

- Computer software and occasionally even hardware is sometimes made available to educational institutions from computer companies wishing to promote their materials among people who will be potential buyers when they graduate.

- When a workshop, course, or program provides direct or indirect service to an industry by training employees or potential employees, the industry may be interested in donating teaching materials and supplies.

- Private individuals, perhaps alumni, may sometimes lend or donate art prints, photograph collections, or text materials to a program or institution.

Summary

Instructional materials communicate messages to students. Most educators rely on books and articles as their primary materials because it is largely through them that they have gained expertise in the discipline. One purpose of this chapter has been to emphasize that there are many alternate forms of materials and each serves a different purpose in relation to the kind of knowledge being acquired.

Instructional materials can be placed on a continuum of concrete to abstract, with the words of books and articles comprising the most abstract form. Photographs and drawings are more concrete because they visually represent objects. Videos and films add motion to the illusion, producing slightly more realism. Models of things provide three dimensions; and sometimes, it is important to work with the real thing as a material.

In addition to being abstract or concrete, materials also vary in who controls the pacing of their use—the teacher, the student, or the producer of the material—and how responsive they are to individual learners. The chalkboard does not talk back, but a real person will, as do some computerized materials. Some instructional materials may not be suited to all group sizes; it is hard for a large group to examine a model or a photograph.

I describe the basic characteristics of commonly used instructional materials, identifying the teaching methods they are usually associated with, the optimal group size for using them, their pacing, and their responsiveness to students. From ordinary spoken words or drawings on a chalkboard to the sophisticated graphics and hyper-linked text available on the Internet, each kind of instructional material has its place.

In order to choose the best material, the requirements of the learning task as stated in the objective are considered first. In order to analyze ideas, students can read about the ideas in a text form and discuss them with others. On the other hand, if the students are to learn to use a particular piece of equipment, they need to work with the real thing—the equipment.

Some student characteristics are relevant in the choice of teaching materials, although what we usually try to do is provide enough variety and choice to accommodate individual preferences. Students with less experience may benefit from more concrete forms of materials, while those with more prior knowledge are more likely to be able to manipulate abstract symbols and concepts. Materials such as directions for assignments and objectives for the day should be provided in both spoken and written form.

Contextual constraints, such as lack of money and resources, may influence the choice of materials. However, there are often innovative ways around these restrictions.

Chapter 7
Evaluating Learning

When it comes to the evaluation of learning even the most experienced instructors have moments of doubt and discomfort. Are we really being fair? Are our grades too high? Too low? How can we really ever know what a student has learned? Should we consider the effort a student puts into a project or just the final result? Can we include student self-evaluation, as recommended in the adult education literature? If students come into a course with different backgrounds, how can we expect them to learn the same amount? How could we tell if they did learn the same amount?

Evaluation is a judgment of the quality or degree of something. Learning is a change in knowledge, skill, or values. Students, teachers, employers, colleagues, and friends and family routinely evaluate learning. When a student says, "I learned a lot in that course," she is evaluating her learning. When a co-worker says, "He's really changed after taking that workshop," this is an evaluation of learning. When an instructor prepares a test or assigns an essay and gives a grade and comments on the learner's work, she is evaluating learning. Evaluation is achieved through informal observations, formal tests, structured observations of performance, discussion, and anecdotal records or comments.

When designing evaluation strategies, the first concern is to decide on the general approach, which depends to a large extent, on the purpose of the evaluation and the teaching context. Next, we need to select evaluation techniques based on the nature of the learning as expressed in the objectives, and, if it is relevant, a grading scheme.

Only then does the teacher prepare tests, assignments, or projects, either for or with the students. In this chapter, I first review general approaches to the evaluation of learning, then give guidelines for selecting specific evaluation techniques. Third, I discuss how to assemble the evaluation techniques into a procedure for assigning grades. Finally, I give detailed suggestions on how to construct good tests, projects, and assignments.

General Approaches to the Evaluation of Learning

Why is learning being evaluated? This is the first thing to ask. Here are some alternative scenarios.

- If, for example, an educator is facilitating a workshop or a non-credit course, which requires no grades, evaluation of learning is usually informal and anecdotal. The educator may ask learners to reflect on and comment on their learning at the end of the workshop or periodically through a non-credit course, but there are no specific tasks or projects that have evaluation as their primary intention.

- Many educators evaluate students because the institution requires grades. These grades may be used by employers for hiring, by administrators to determine whether students can go on to another course, or by other institutions to decide who goes to graduate school. Evaluation is more formal and is usually based on specific tasks, tests, or learning projects.

- Teachers often evaluate students with the intention of improving instruction and learning. The goal is to see what people have learned so that further instruction, clarification, or review can be provided.

- The purpose of evaluation may be to ensure that students meet certain standards. In health education or trades training, for example, evaluation procedures ensure that graduates can care for patients or repair expensive industrial equipment. In this case, it is not necessary to compare students to each other, but rather to determine that everyone is competent.

There are at least three available approaches to evaluation; our choice among these will depend on the purpose of our evaluation. These alternatives are informal or formal, norm-referenced or criterion-referenced, and student self-evaluated or teacher evaluated. In many contexts, more than one evaluation approach is used.

Formal and Informal Evaluation By formal evaluation, I mean those evaluations that contribute to marks, grades, or official records, including pass/fail tests or situations. Formal evaluations usually accompany courses, workshops, or programs that are accredited. Students receive credit toward a degree or certificate for having completed the instruction.

Informal evaluations serve to provide feedback to further learning, but do not become official in any way and are not accessible by other individuals, such as administrators or employers. Informal evaluation, or feedback, should always be a part of a teaching and learning experience regardless of whether or not formal evaluation procedures are in place.

Formal evaluations, because they need to be quantified — turned into percentages, letter grades or pass/fail marks — usually involve testing where we can count the number of correct answers or rate the quality of responses. Informal evaluation requires no quantification and therefore usually is more anecdotal. Verbal comments or written feedback contribute to informal evaluations.

Norm-referenced and Criterion-referenced Evaluation Formal evaluations may be either norm-or criterion-referenced, or some combination of the two. Norm-referenced evaluation compares individuals to a norm. A true norm-referenced test is one that has been given to a very large sample of people, encompassing certain ages, educational backgrounds, and possibly, cultures. Averages or norms are obtained for all responses within certain demographic categories — a procedure called standardization. Then, when the same test is given to an individual student, we can say, for example, that Sam is above the norm in verbal intelligence for his age group, but below the norm in spatial intelligence. Entrance examinations, certification examinations, and aptitude inventories are other examples of traditional norm-referenced evaluations. Two critical assumptions underlie this approach: ability or achievement is normally distributed in the population, and the sample upon which the instrument was standardized is an adequate representation of the population. The concept of normal distribution has specific statistical properties, but for our purposes, it is enough to understand that it means that most people cluster around the middle or average, and a few obtain very high and very low results.

When instructors use norm-referenced testing, they usually do not standardize their tests. That is, they do not administer the test to large samples, develop norms, and compare individual students to the norm. Instead, they take the average of a class or group as the norm and compare individuals within that same group to the average. Based on a norm-referenced approach, instructors can say, "The learner is above the mean for this test," "The individual is in the top 10% of the group," or "This person has performed better than that person." Sometimes instructors "grade on a curve," meaning that they use the concept of a normal distribution to assign grades. Very few people receive high or low grades; most receive average grades *regardless of the actual test results*.

There are two serious problems with instructor-designed, norm-referenced evaluations. One is that there is no reason to assume that learning in our classes has a classic normal distribution. In fact, we have lots of good reasons, including a belief in the quality of our teaching, to assume that learning would not be normally distributed. The second problem is that the evaluation techniques used are not standardized so the average of a particular class is used as the norm. Since every group is different, the "norms" fluctuate from one group to another and lose their meaning.

The purpose of criterion-referenced evaluation is to determine whether or not individuals meet a certain pre-specified criterion or standard. Evaluation is usually focused on the acquisition of technical or instrumental knowledge. Test scores are compared to a cut-off score, which has been selected as indicative of mastery of the content. Traditional published criterion-referenced tests are short, about 10 items long, and designed to assess learning of a specific objective. Passing the test—meeting the criterion—allows students to go on to the next objective.

When instructors choose a criterion-referenced approach, they do so because they have no need to compare students. They are interested only in being able to say, "This individual has (or has not) mastered this objective or set of objectives." In a pure criterion-referenced approach, no allowance is made for degrees of quality in student performance.

The assumptions underlying criterion-referenced evaluation are that the acquisition of knowledge is a yes/no phenomenon and it can be objectively assessed. When educators are working in the lower levels of the cognitive domain and all but the highest level of the psychomotor domain, they may be able to make this assumption. Otherwise, with more complex cognitive knowledge or any learning in the affective domain, they cannot.

Although most of us do not use pure norm-or criterion-referenced evaluation techniques, it is important to understand their underlying assumptions. If educators use some mixture of criterion-and norm-based testing, they need to be clear as to what that mixture is and what that purpose is in including each. Do they need to compare people? Can they actually define mastery?

Instructor Evaluation and Student Self-Evaluation Both formal and informal evaluation procedures may include either student self-evaluation or instructor evaluation, or some combination of the two. Instructor evaluation is common in most settings. The instructor is always responsible for giving feedback, although students may give each other feedback during discussions and group projects. More importantly, in most people's eyes, the instructor is the one who gives grades, ratings, and comments on students' work. The assumption underlying this approach is that the instructor, who has the subject-area expertise, is the person best able to judge students' learning and development.

Student self-evaluation is recommended in the adult education literature for a variety of reasons. This proposal is based on the assumption that adult learners prefer to be self-directed in their learning and, as a part of that process, are capable of evaluating their own progress toward their goals. In some domains of learning, it is unlikely that an instructor knows as well as the learner the changes she has made. It is only the learner who can truly speak to values development, for example, or changes in personal perspectives. Self-evaluation also has to do with issues of power in the relationship between teacher and learner. If students are being encouraged to become autonomous, independent learners and yet the instructor maintains the power of assigning marks, full student autonomy cannot be achieved.

The use of student self-evaluation raises some complex questions, especially in contexts where formal evaluation is required. Many students have not engaged in self-evaluation and therefore may not have the skills to do so. They may feel anxious about being asked to evaluate their own learning, when they are used to the teacher telling them how they are doing. Self-evaluation may be questionable in disciplines where the knowledge is primarily technical in nature and where a certain level of technical competence needs to be guaranteed. Students here may not be able to judge the amount or quality of their learning simply because they have little expertise in the subject.

Student self-evaluation need not be an all-or-nothing approach. Students can participate in some aspects of evaluating their learning but not others. They can help set criteria or standards for evaluation, they can participate in determining how various components of the course will be weighed in a final grade, or they can evaluate one part of their learning and leave other parts for the teacher's judgment.

Here, I suggest some strategies for facilitating self-evaluation.

- Students need to learn how to do self-evaluations. Educators should spend time helping them gain these skills.
- Students can assist each other in pairs or small groups in self-evaluation.
- Educators can meet with students individually to discuss their self-evaluation plans.
- Students should be encouraged to use different formats to gather evidence of their learning.
- Self-evaluation can include a validation of the evidence of learning. Students may do this through presentations to peers, discussions with the instructor, or consultations with professionals or colleagues.

- Journals or logbooks are useful aids for student self-evaluation.
- Final course grades should be determined during individual consultations between the student and the instructor.

The decision whether or not to use instructor or student self-evaluation should be based on careful reflection. Is it suitable for the subject? Are students able and willing to evaluate their own learning? What are the consequences for the institution or the profession involved?

Selecting Evaluation Techniques

Evaluation techniques should be based on the nature of the expected learning. Evaluation techniques provide evidence of learning; therefore, the evaluation task must allow for the expression of the kind of learning involved. A multiple-choice test does not allow for the expression of communicative abilities, for example. Conversely, an essay does not allow for a comprehensive survey of remembered facts. Other important factors are: practical considerations, such as group size, facilities, time limitations, or certification requirements; and learner characteristics, such as verbal ability, special needs, or previous test experience. But, the type of learning must be considered first; then, if necessary, techniques can be chosen or modified that will accommodate other factors.

Two broad categories of evaluation techniques are linked to the nature of learning: objectively scored and subjectively rated. Objectively scored techniques are those in which two people using the same scoring key would always agree on the results. These include multiple-choice items, true/false items, matching tests, some short answer questions, and some checklists. Subjectively rated techniques are those that involve interpretation on the part of the evaluator. These include some short answer questions, essays, oral tests, most checklists, rating scales, and anecdotal records or comments.

Learning that is concrete, technical, or instrumental in nature is best evaluated by objectively scored techniques. The lower levels of the cognitive domain fall into this realm. Although much psychomotor learning is also technical or instrumental in nature, it is impossible to directly represent it with paper-and-pencil instruments. Psychomotor learning is demonstrated in a physical performance, which must then be observed by someone or reported on by the learner. Learning that is communicative or emancipatory in nature is acquired when people construct knowledge through discussion and interaction with others. It is interpretive in nature. When there are no definite right answers, educators use subjectively rated evaluation techniques, those that allow for interpretation. The higher levels of the cognitive domain and most of the affective domain include learning of this nature.

Considering Domains and Levels of Learning

Table 7-1presents a matrix of the cognitive levels of learning by testing techniques. Each type of test is described as "always appropriate" for the level of learning (Yes), "can be appropriate in

Table 7-1. Appropriateness of Testing Techniques in the Cognitive Domain.

Types of Tests / Levels of Domain	Multiple Choice	True/False	Matching	Short Answer	Essay Test	Oral Test	Checklist	Rating Scale	Comments, Anecdotal Records
Knowledge	Yes	Yes	Yes	Yes	No	No	Maybe	No	Maybe
Comprehension	Yes	Yes	Yes	Yes	No	No	Maybe	No	Maybe
Application	Yes	No	No	Yes	Maybe	Maybe	Maybe	Maybe	Yes
Analysis	Maybe	No	No	Maybe	Yes	Yes	No	Maybe	Yes
Synthesis	No	No	No	No	Yes	Yes	No	Maybe	Yes
Evaluation	No	No	No	No	Yes	Yes	No	Maybe	Yes

Yes = Always appropriate
Maybe = Can be appropriate in some situations
No = Never appropriate

some situations" (Maybe), or "never appropriate" (No). Sometimes several evaluation formats are labeled as "always appropriate" for some levels of learning. Any of the objectively scored tests are appropriate for the knowledge and comprehension levels of the cognitive domain. The choice of format depends only on the instructor's or the student's preferences or characteristics. Where the testing technique is described as "can be appropriate in some situations," the decision depends on the subject, level of instruction, student characteristics, or even instructor skill in preparing items.

All objectively scored evaluation techniques—multiple choice, true/false, matching, short answer questions—are appropriate for the knowledge and comprehension levels. True/false items and matching items do not work well for the application level; on these kinds of tests, students only have to recognize what they have learned, not apply their knowledge to new situations. Nor can objectively scored techniques be used to evaluate higher-level cognitive learning, where students are analyzing and interpreting knowledge. When there are no right answers, it is not appropriate to use a test format that asks for right answers. Of the subjectively rated techniques, essays and oral formats can assess higher-level cognitive learning. Checklists and rating scales are designed for evaluating an observed performance. However, in a field setting, when a student is able to diagnose and repair a piece of heavy equipment, we can assume that he or she has the underlying cognitive knowledge necessary to perform the repair. Comments and anecdotal notes can provide feedback in informal evaluations in the cognitive domain or be used similarly to rating scales in field or clinical settings.

Table 7-2 develops the same matrix for the levels of learning in the affective domain. Here, objectively scored techniques may be useful at the lower levels, though there are probably better ways to find out if people have been exposed to and responded to a value than a multiple-choice question. It is unlikely that either true/false or matching items would be used at all. The essay and oral test formats are appropriate at the higher levels of learning. Observation techniques (checklists, rating scales, anecdotal records) are generally useful.

Types of Tests	Multiple Choice	True/False	Matching	Short Answer	Essay Test	Oral Test	Checklist	Rating Scale	Comments, Anecdotal Records
Levels of Domain									
Receiving	Maybe	No	No	Yes	No	No	Yes	No	Yes
Responding	Maybe	No	No	Maybe	Maybe	Maybe	Yes	No	Yes
Valuing	Maybe	No	No	No	Yes	Yes	Yes	Yes	Yes
Organization	No	No	No	No	Yes	Yes	No	Yes	Yes
Value complex	No	No	No	No	Yes	Yes	No	Yes	Yes

Table 7-2. Appropriateness of Testing Techniques in the Affective Domain.

Yes = Always appropriate
Maybe = Can be appropriate in some situations
No = Never appropriate

Table 7-3 offers a matrix of testing techniques for psychomotor levels of learning. None of the paper and pencil techniques are appropriate here. Whether or not a student correctly answers a question about a psychomotor performance on paper has nothing to do with whether or not he or she can actually perform. It cannot be assumed that students are able to translate knowledge into action. I may answer correctly any number of test questions on carburetors, but still be unable to clean or recondition one. A physical performance needs to be observed to be evaluated. Either checklists or rating scales can be used for this purpose. In addition, comments and anecdotal notes are useful for giving feedback to students after watching them perform. Or students can keep notes on their performance, describing what they did, and discuss this later with the instructor or other students to obtain feedback. Comments and anecdotal notes can be incorporated into formal evaluations as well in the psychomotor domain. I discuss this application when I review the different evaluation techniques in detail.

Table 7-3. Appropriateness of Testing Techniques in the Psychomotor Domain.									
Types of Tests	Multiple Choice	True/False	Matching	Short Answer	Essay Test	Oral Test	Checklist	Rating Scale	Comments, Anecdotal Records
Levels of Domain									
Perception	No	No	No	No	No	No	Maybe	Maybe	Maybe
Simulation	No	No	No	No	No	No	Yes	Yes	Maybe
Conformation	No	No	No	No	No	No	Yes	Yes	Yes
Production	No	No	No	No	No	No	Yes	Yes	Yes
Mastery	No	No	No	No	No	No	Yes	Yes	Yes

Yes = Always appropriate
Maybe = Can be appropriate in some situations
No = Never appropriate

Practical Considerations Sometimes, the ideal evaluation tool must be modified because of practical considerations. Group size, facilities and resources, time constraints, and the requirements of professional associations or certification boards all may influence the choice of evaluation techniques.

With a class of over 50 people, subjectively rated evaluations take a lot of time. Some people are willing to devote this time to their teaching, and we must applaud their dedication, but we cannot reasonably expect teachers to spend all of their evenings and weekends reading essays. In some contexts, the following suggestions may be helpful.

- We might be able to use more structured, shorter essay questions with a relatively simple and straightforward scoring system.

- If teaching assistants are available or can be obtained, they can help read essays. This, of course, implies that the assistants have been given clear criteria upon which to base evaluation and are familiar enough with the subject and topic to do so accurately and fairly, and make meaningful comments.

- Students can read and comment on each other's essays. Clear, agreed-upon criteria should be used. We can read a sample of the essays each time, adding our own comments to those of the students.

- We can use short answer or multiple-choice items to assess all of the lower level cognitive components of the learning, then use only one or two short essay questions to evaluate the integration or analysis of these ideas.

Facilities and resources may be an important consideration when we are evaluating psychomotor learning where it is essential to see each student's performance. In a clinical setting, students may be spread out all over the hospital or social service agency, each performing different tasks at different times. If a laboratory is short of equipment, students may need to double up to conduct experiments. Here are a few ways to work around such constraints.

- Simulations or role plays can be used to evaluate performance, keeping in mind that performance in a real setting will be somewhat different.

- When there is a shortage of equipment, students can work in pairs. One person can perform one task while the other evaluates, then students reverse roles for the next task.

- Learners can work in small groups to complete a project using the same material, equipment, or resources, and evaluation can focus on the group's performance.

- When we are unable to observe individual performances, students can keep journals, recording what they do and commenting on their problems, reactions, and successes.

As mentioned above, time is a consideration when reading essays from large groups and also can be a factor in other contexts. If checklists or rating scales are used to evaluate psychomotor learning, each student is assessed separately. If the performance is long or complex, this requires a great deal of time. In other contexts, an appropriate evaluation strategy may involve excessive student time. In a research course, is it reasonable to expect students actually to conduct research? In a carpentry course, is there time to have students demonstrate all the techniques they have learned by constructing a building? Often compromises are necessary.

- Rather than evaluating each student's entire performance, we can sample the performance of individuals while several people are engaged in the same task.
- When the product of a performance accurately reflects what a learner does, we can examine that product rather than observing the entire process.
- In cases where a large number of detailed lower-level steps are required in a performance, we can look only at the final steps and conclude that the previous steps were done correctly.

In some contexts, the requirements of professional associations or certification boards need to be taken into account. For example, in a trades program, the students may be working with higher-level cognitive skills or psychomotor skills and therefore subjectively rated evaluation techniques are used, but the certification examination may have a multiple-choice format. In order to prepare students for the certification process, they should have the opportunity to practice responding to the test format.

- To prepare learners for a particular test format, that type of test can be used, but not included in the grading scheme.
- Required test formats can be combined with the preferred format, but be given less weight in the grading scheme.
- We should always promote good evaluation. We can lobby professional associations, external agencies, and administrators to make changes.

Considering Learner Characteristics I discuss, in Chapters Five and Six, how learner characteristics should be considered in the selection of teaching methods and materials. At times, it is important to consider the preferences and needs of students when we select evaluation strategies as well. Some adults, especially if they have been away from education for a while, are very anxious and threatened by evaluation. We should always check how familiar students are with a specific test format. People who are quite comfortable writing essays can become paralyzed at the sight of a multiple-choice test, and vice versa. For introverted people, performing psychomotor skills while being evaluated may cause them to forget all they have learned. Sometimes, students working in a second language or those with lower literacy skills need special consideration.

- Educators should find out how students feel about the planned evaluation strategies. Discussing the strategies with them, asking for their suggestions, and being flexible are important.
- When students are not familiar with or are especially uncomfortable with an evaluation format, practice sessions can be provided and supportive feedback given.
- When students are writing in their second language, educators can give feedback on grammar and spelling mistakes but not consider them in the grading.
- Sometimes educators can have an interview or discussion with a student who has difficulty writing, that is, use an oral test rather than an essay test.

Planning a Grading System

I am certain I have never met an educator who enjoys assigning grades. We like our students and want them to learn and do well. What a dilemma it is when someone's essay or project is disappointing, and yet we know how hard she worked on it. If only we did not need to give grades. Yet, grades are required in many settings and do serve a purpose. They communicate something about a student's learning to that student, other instructors, administrators, and potential employers. They reward, motivate, and reinforce many students. They are often an essential part of selection processes—for graduate school or medical school, and for awards and scholarships.

Here, I review the common approaches to grading and give some guidelines for planning a grading system. Galbraith and Jones (2010) distinguish between norm-referenced and criterion referenced models of assessment. In the norm-referenced model, grades are assigned on the basis of students' relative standing in a group.

Students may be ranked based on evaluation results. This model is only appropriate when people need to be differentiated from each other and therefore is not often used in adult education settings.

In the criterion-referenced model, grades are assigned on the basis of mastery of a set of objectives. Criterion-referenced evaluation may lead to a pass/fail grading system or may be modified to include a small number of categories in order to meet institutional requirements. Cut-off points (criteria) for the grades are planned in advance, learners receive a grade that reflects their mastery of the objectives.

Contract grading is a fairly common model in adult education. The instructor and student negotiate and come to an agreement on the quality and quantity of work required for a specific grade. For example, they might decide that if the student attends all sessions and participates in all activities, a grade of C will be given; if, in addition, he chooses to write two essays on a relevant topic, a grade of B will be given, and if he presents one paper to the group, he will get an A. Contracts can also be based on the growth or improvement a person demonstrates. The great advantage of this model is that the learners have control over their grades. There are some problems with contracts, however. Some students find them restrictive: as they learn more about a subject, they develop new interests and want to do something different. We need to be sure that students know that contracts can be flexible. A major disadvantage of contracts is that it is hard to build in a way to recognize the quality of the student's work.

Student self-evaluation, as described earlier in this chapter, can also be used as a grading model. Students set criteria for their work in consultation with the instructor, validate their work with another person, and assign themselves a grade.

In some contexts, educators develop a weighting system for grading, where the different components of the course or session are given different values in terms of the contribution they make to the final grade. Weights can be based on such aspects as the amount of time spent on the objectives represented and the importance of the learning. For example, in professional training, there is usually a set of essential skills, which must be acquired. If an essential skill is not mastered, the decision might be that a student must not pass, regardless of his performance on other objectives. And, similarly, whenever objectives are prerequisites for later learning or necessary for certification, they may have more weight in the grading scheme. Or, higher levels of learning may be given more weight than the lower levels.

It can be useful to devise a matrix of objectives by evaluation techniques, indicating the time spent on each objective by the learners and the importance of that objective in terms of the training, program, or future learning. This will ensure that the evaluation of each objective is considered in the grading plan, and that the time spent and the importance of the learning are a part of the scheme.

The final consideration in planning a grading system is how we combine the various evaluation results. A score of 60 on a test where the scores range from 50 to 65 does not have the same meaning as a score of 60 on a test where the scores range from 35 to 60. It is best to convert scores to a common denominator such as a percentage out of 100.

Designing Evaluation Techniques

In this section, I describe in detail each of the evaluation techniques and give guidelines for constructing good questions or items.

Multiple-Choice Tests The multiple-choice test is the most common of the objectively scored formats. An item consists of a statement or question, called the stem, followed by a set of alternative endings to the statement or answers to the question. The wrong choices are called *distractors*, as they are designed to draw the student who does not have the knowledge away from the right answer. There are usually three or four distractors in each item. Items should have clear, unambiguous stems with correct answers that are not a matter of opinion or controversy. The distractors should be short, plausible, and grammatically consistent with each other and the stem. The correct answer should be clearly right, not merely close or best.

Multiple-choice tests can efficiently assess learning for a large number of objectives. They are quick to score. However, good multiple-choice items are difficult and time-consuming to construct. They encourage students to guess and do not provide an opportunity for people to elaborate on their response. They cannot be used to evaluate learning in higher cognitive domain levels— analysis, synthesis, evaluation—or learning in affective or psychomotor domains.

Example 1:

> Why do living organisms need oxygen?
>> a. to purify the blood
>>
>> b. to oxidize waste
>>
>> d. to assimilate food
>>
>> e. to fight infection

This item has a question as the stem. The alternatives are grammatically parallel, short, and all will be plausible to the learner who does not know the answer.

Example 2:

> The objective, "The student will be able to write a critique of John Fowles' *Mantissa*, based on the criteria of effective style, plot development and characterization" is an example of:
>> a. knowledge level learning
>>
>> b. analysis level learning
>>
>> c. synthesis level learning
>>
>> d. evaluation level learning

This example contains an incomplete statement as a stem.

The most difficult part of writing good multiple-choice items is to generate plausible distractors. It is a good idea to have a colleague or former student review multiple-choice items. Even a person who is not familiar with the subject can be helpful. If she can find the right answer, in spite of not knowing it, the item is faulty.

Following are some guidelines for constructing good items.

- Present one clearly stated problem, statement, or question in the stem of the item.
- Use simple, clear language with no subjective words, such as "best," or controversial concepts.
- Put as much as possible of the wording into the stem of the item, so as to avoid redundant or complex distractors.
- State the stem in a positive form. If negative wording must be used, emphasize it by underlining or capitalizing the negative words.
- Ensure that all alternatives are grammatically consistent with the stem.
- Avoid any verbal clues that might enable learners to select the correct answer or eliminate incorrect alternatives.
- Develop distractors that are plausible and attractive to the learner who does not know the answer.
- Vary the relative length of the correct alternative. We have a tendency to add extra qualifications to the right answer.
- Vary the position of the correct answer.
- Avoid the use of "all of the above" as an alternative: it is generally not the correct answer, and if it is, the item format should be a short answer.
- Avoid the use of "none of the above" as an alternative: it is rarely the correct answer, and when it is, there is no certainty that learners do know the right answer.
- Design each item so that it is independent of other items on the test and contains no clues to answers for other items.

True/False Tests A true/false test consists of a series of statements which students label as true or false. The statements must be concise, straightforward, and clear statements of fact, without qualifiers, opinions, or values. Since guessing the answer is obviously a disadvantage of using this format, some variations have been developed in which students are asked to explain why the item is false or to underline those words or phrases that make the statement false. Some people advocate a "right minus wrong" scoring technique to discourage guessing, but this tends to increase test anxiety.

True/false tests efficiently assess the learning of a large number of objectives and are quick to score. However, the guessing factor decreases the accuracy of the evaluation. True or false items are only appropriate for the knowledge or comprehension levels of the cognitive domain.

Example 1:

> If the discriminant is negative, a quadratic equation has no real roots.
>
> T   F

This item illustrates a straightforward, factual statement in which there is no ambiguity or opinion. The objective would be at the comprehension level of the cognitive domain.

Example 2:

> In the year 800 C.E., Julius Caesar was crowned Emperor of the Holy Roman Empire. (If false, underline the word(s) that make the statement false).
>
> T   F

In this example, asking students to underline the part of the statement that makes it false counteracts the effect of guessing. There are several phrases that could be false: the date, the person, the title, or the verb "was crowned."

True/false items are fairly easy to create. Here are some guidelines.

- In each statement, include only one concept, which is clearly true or false.
- Keep the statement short, using simple language without complex grammatical structures.
- Use negative statements sparingly and never use double negatives.
- Avoid the use of qualifying words or phrases (e.g. "all," "never," "often").

• Attribute statements of opinion to a specific source.

Matching Tests   A matching test consists of two columns of names, dates, or definitions which must be correctly matched. One item from one column always matches a corresponding item in the second column. There should be different numbers of items in each column to discourage guessing by elimination.

Matching tests are easy to score and fairly easy to design. They only evaluate learning at the knowledge and comprehension levels of the cognitive domain.

Example 1:

For each of the European novelists listed below on the left side, choose the title of the corresponding novel and put the appropriate letter beside the author's name.

__ 1. Turgenev	a. Buddenbrooks
__ 2. Hesse	b. Germinal
__ 3. Malraux	c. Fathers and Sons
__ 4. Mann	d. Nausea
__ 5. Silone	e. Bread and Wine
__ 6. Tolstoy	f. Steppenwolf
__ 7. Zola	g. Brothers Karamazov
__ 8. Camus	h. Man's Fate
	i. The Outsider
	j. War and Peace
	k. Madame Bovary

This example illustrates a straightforward matching of titles and authors. Learning at the knowledge level of the cognitive domain is being evaluated. More titles than authors are listed, and the incorrect titles are plausible.

Example 2:

For each of the terms listed on the left, select the appropriate definition and place the letter next to the term.

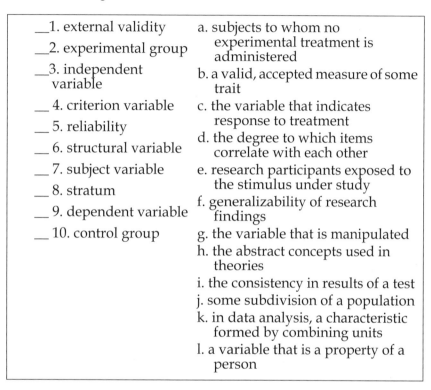

__1. external validity	a. subjects to whom no experimental treatment is administered
__2. experimental group	
__3. independent variable	b. a valid, accepted measure of some trait
__ 4. criterion variable	c. the variable that indicates response to treatment
__ 5. reliability	d. the degree to which items correlate with each other
__ 6. structural variable	e. research participants exposed to the stimulus under study
__ 7. subject variable	f. generalizability of research findings
__ 8. stratum	g. the variable that is manipulated
__ 9. dependent variable	h. the abstract concepts used in theories
__ 10. control group	i. the consistency in results of a test
	j. some subdivision of a population
	k. in data analysis, a characteristic formed by combining units
	l. a variable that is a property of a person

This example illustrates a slightly more complex use of the matching item. It can evaluate learning at the comprehension level of the cognitive domain. Several different concepts—types of variables, reliability, validity—are included so it is important that the list of definitions contain plausible distractors and also essential that the wording does not allow students to make the correct match without understanding the concept. Below are some suggestions for creating clear matching items.

- Use homogeneous lists in each column of the item, for example, historical events and the relevant dates, authors and titles, terms and definitions. If each list is not homogeneous, students can eliminate incorrect responses.

- Use between five and fifteen items on each list. Fewer items allow guessing, and more become confusing.

- Arrange the response list, which is usually on the right hand side, in alphabetical or chronological order to facilitate the finding of the correct alternative.

- Clearly indicate in the directions the basis upon which the matching is to be done.

- Have unequal numbers of items in the two lists in order to minimize guessing.

Short Answer Tests The objectively scored, short answer item consists of either a question for which only one word or phrase is the correct response or a statement in which the student fills in missing words or phrases. If it is to be objectively scored, the short answer must be unambiguously correct or incorrect.

Short answer items require students to produce the correct answer, rather than merely recognize it. They usually evaluate learning at the comprehension level of the cognitive domain. When used to present problems to be solved in mathematics or statistics, short answer items evaluate learning at the application level of the cognitive domain. They are easy to prepare and score and are commonly used for those reasons.

Example 1:

According to Cranton (2011), the six levels of learning in the cognitive domain are:

_____

_____

_____

_____

_____

_____

This example is a statement-completion item to evaluate learning at the knowledge or comprehension level of the cognitive domain. The authority upon which the information is based is cited and the number of responses is specified.

Example 2:

> Calculate (rounding to one decimal point) the mean and standard deviation of the following set of test scores: 42, 57, 66, 66, 68, 72, 75, 75, 91.
>
> Mean: _____ Standard deviation: _____

This item evaluates learning at the application level of the cognitive domain. If students are asked to show their work and if some marks are given for the process students use, instructor judgment is needed, and the item would be subjectively rated.

Following are some guidelines for writing short answer items.

- Write the question or statement so that a correct answer is clear.
- Limit the length of the response to single words or short phrases. Longer responses usually result in subjective scoring.
- In incomplete statements, only omit significant or keywords or phrases.
- Do not provide grammatical clues as to the correct response.
- When using the incomplete statement format, construct the statement so that the blank appears near the end. It is hard to hold a statement in our mind when a word is missing near the beginning.
- Avoid using verbatim quotes from a textbook or reading.
- Prepare a scoring key that includes all possible correct answers.

Essays The essay is the most commonly used subjectively rated evaluation technique. Essays are written in formal testing situations or are used as assignments or learning projects. They can range greatly in length, from a short or restricted format requiring a paragraph, outline, or few pages to a longer or unrestricted format yielding a paper of 50 or more pages. In a classroom test, essays may be completed either with or without the use of resource materials. When essays are written outside of the classroom, pairs or small groups may work on them.

Essays evaluate learning at the higher levels of the cognitive and affective domains. They allow for an in-depth examination of the students' understanding of a topic or subject. People can express personal opinions and individual ideas, and elaborate on aspects of a topic in which they are interested. Several objectives can often be evaluated with one analytical or integrative essay topic. Essay questions are fairly easy to write. On the downside, marking essays and providing feedback on them takes time. Sometimes, too, we are influenced by our own opinion on the topic or our feelings and expectations about the student.

Example 1:

> Assuming that your reader has a background in psychoanalytic theory, describe in five to ten pages how Jung's ideas deviated from those of his mentor, Sigmund Freud. Where necessary, give references (a useful source is the Freud-Jung letters, distributed in class).

This item illustrates an unrestricted essay format, evaluating learning at the analysis level of the cognitive domain. Students are told clearly what is expected and material is suggested.

Example 2:

> Describe in one paragraph each, the lecture and the discussion methods of teaching (no more than 200 words per paragraph). Include in your descriptions, examples of an instructional situation in which each method is appropriate.

This example is of the restricted essay type. There is little room for speculation or opinion. Application level learning in the cognitive domain is being evaluated.

Example 3:

> As a nursing student, you are caring for an elderly patient who is terminally ill with lung cancer. He is in pain and refuses to take his medication, which you know is essential for life. How would you respond to this patient?

Like Example 1, this item is unrestricted in format. It is evaluating learning at the valuing level in the affective domain. Students are free to express feelings and devise unique strategies for dealing with the situation.

Although essay questions are relatively simple to prepare, the rating or scoring process needs attention. Below are some suggestions for creating good essay questions.

- Design each question to evaluate one or more well-defined learning outcomes.

- Present a clear, unambiguous task to students.

- Include in the question any conditions or criteria, such as length, format, and grammatical or spelling requirements.

- Avoid the use of jargon and complex sentence structures.

- In advance, outline the types of things that should be included in each response.

- Using the outline as a guide, devise a rating system in which students receive marks for concepts, arguments, or other relevant attributes.

- Evaluate all students' responses to one question before proceeding to the next question. This helps to minimize the quality of one response affecting the perception of the next.

- Give detailed written comments, addressing both the strengths of the work and areas that could be improved.

Oral Tests Oral tests consist of a series of structured or semi-structured questions or a single question to which students respond verbally. Sometimes the answers are tape-recorded so they can be reviewed. In formal situations, such as comprehensive examinations in graduate school, more than one instructor or examiner may be present. Oral tests are commonly used both formally and informally in second language learning. Generally, oral evaluations can take the form of interviews, discussions, or presentations. They evaluate learning at the higher levels of the cognitive and affective domains.

Oral evaluations allow for an in-depth examination of learners' understanding and provide an opportunity for the expression of opinions and an elaboration on points of interest. When the course objectives address speaking ability, as they might in social work, leadership, or management, oral tests are especially valuable. The rating of an oral performance is difficult, however. Although checklists or rating scales can be useful, their use tends to detract from the spontaneity of the interaction. Oral evaluations are also anxiety-provoking for students.

Example 1:

> Self-directed learning was originally viewed as a method by which students made decisions about objectives, resources, and evaluation techniques in a systematic instructional design model. In recent years, self-directed learning has been viewed as a political concept, one fostering empowerment and freedom from oppression. Do you agree with one of these perspectives more than the other? Can you reconcile the two perspectives?

> Take about ten minutes to discuss your views on self-directed learning in adult education. At the end of your discussion, the committee will have the opportunity to ask you further questions.

This example provides a clear topic for discussion and yet allows an unrestricted response. The student is free to state opinions and develop points of interest. At the end of the presentation, an opportunity is provided for evaluators to probe or ask further questions.

Example 2:

> In the group to which you have been assigned (four individuals per group), discuss the following issue: how would you, in your social work field experience, counsel an unmarried woman of 26 years of age who was deciding whether to undergo a tubal ligation? Discuss the characteristics of the client's lifestyle that might influence your counseling. You have fifteen minutes.

This example illustrates the use of interaction among learners. Although evaluation of individuals is more difficult, students feel less anxious and are stimulated by the discussion with their peers.

Some guidelines for the preparation and rating of oral presentations follow.

- Present students with a clear, well-defined task that is directly related to one or more objectives.

- Prepare questions that are comparable in length and difficulty.

- Circulate copies of the questions to students in advance of the evaluation.
- Clearly indicate how long the answers should be.
- During a discussion or interview, use probing questions carefully so as not to lead participants to the expected responses.
- Establish a comfortable, relaxed atmosphere to minimize anxiety.
- Tape-record or videotape the session, or take good notes.
- Develop criteria for rating the answers based on the objectives being evaluated.
- Consider converting the criteria into a checklist or rating scale for use during or after the evaluation.
- In formal evaluations, especially when important decisions are being made, consider having more than one person rate student responses.

Checklists Checklists are most commonly used to evaluate psychomotor skills where a performance or the product of a performance is being assessed. They can also be used in the affective domain, especially at the lower levels. A checklist is an aid to recording the occurrence or frequency of occurrence of behaviors or attributes of a product. It is a list of behaviors or characteristics which are checked off as they are observed. A checklist does not provide for any judgments of quality—it has a simple yes/no format.

Example 1:

	Met	Not Met
1. All caries and defective areas removed.	____	____
2. Cavity preparation is clean.	____	____
3. Adjacent tooth is undamaged.	____	____

This example is a segment of a checklist used in a pre-clinical dental course. Students have completed a procedure and the instructor, using a ten-item checklist, examines the product of their work. The skills have clear standards of acceptability.

Example 2:

_____ 1. Doctor's orders are checked.

_____ 2. Name of drug is checked.

_____ 3. Time that drug is to be given is checked.

_____ 4. Amount of drug to be given is checked.

_____ 5. Method of giving drug is checked.

_____ 6. Patient's name is checked.

This example is an excerpt from a checklist used to evaluate students administering a medication in a college-level nursing course. The listed behaviors occur or they do not. There is no quality of performance involved.

Checklists are relatively easy to prepare and use. Below are some guidelines.

• Write short, clear, unambiguous items which are not open to more than one interpretation on the part of the observer.

• Include only one behavior or characteristic in each item.

• Design each item so that it is answerable in a yes/no format.

• Keep the number of items to a minimum. Checklists containing more than 15 items become unmanageable to use.

• Organize items in a logical or chronological sequence to facilitate use.

Rating Scales   Rating scales are used when we are concerned with the quality of performance in the psychomotor domain or when we require indicators of affective learning. This tool consists of a list of behaviors, attributes, or characteristics expressed in observable terms, accompanied by a scale, such as "Outstanding, Good, Satisfactory, Poor" or "Always, Often, Sometimes, Never."

Rating scales allow the evaluation of several aspects of a performance during one observation or session. They are relatively easy to prepare and use, but are open to quite a bit of interpretation. Two people watching the same performance will almost always see different things and give somewhat different ratings.

Example 1:

Indicate the extent to which you agree or disagree with each of the statements listed below. Consider only the performance which you are observing on this occasion.

Scale:
1. Strongly Disagree 2. Disagree 3. Agree 4. Strongly Agree

The student teacher:

1. Responds clearly to questions.	1 2 3 4
2. States expectations of students.	1 2 3 4
3. Distinguishes between major and minor topics.	1 2 3 4
4. Summarizes major topics.	1 2 3 4

This example is a segment of a rating scale used in the evaluation of student teachers' performance in the classroom. The evaluator is rating the student teacher using a four-point scale. The items may include judgmental words such as "clearly," as in Item 1.

Example 2:

1. Outline of occlusal portion is rounded with no sharp curves.	A B C D E
2. Dimension of occlusal outline and isthmus is 1/4 intercuspal distance.	A B C D E
3. Pulpal depth is 1.5 to 2.0 mm.	A B C D E
4. Each cavity wall of proximal portion clears adjacent tooth by 0.25 to 0.5 mm.	A B C D E

Scale:

A: *Unacceptable.* A significant error is made and cannot be corrected.

B: *Satisfactory.* There is a significant error, which is biologically or mechanically detrimental, but it can be corrected. Minimally clinically acceptable.

C: *Satisfactory.* An error is detected which is not biologically or mechanically detrimental. The error is clinically acceptable but uncorrectable, or clinically unacceptable, but readily correctable.

D: *Satisfactory.* An error is detected that slightly departs from the ideal.

E: *Excellent.* There is no discernible error.

This example is a segment of a rating scale used in a pre-clinical dentistry course. The scale is specific to the content. The usual order of letters used, A through E, is reversed in an attempt to avoid a rater "response set" (i.e., a reliance on preconceived meanings for the points on a scale).

Example 3:

For each of the following statements, indicate the extent to which you agree or disagree using the scale given. Please indicate honestly how *you feel.*

Scale:

1. Strongly Disagree 2. Disagree 3. Agree 4. Strongly Agree

1. I feel responsible for any mistakes I make. 1 2 3 4

2. If I don't like people, I would have   1 2 3 4
   trouble interacting with them
   professionally.

3. If someone asked me a specific question 1 2 3 4
   about a patient, I would most likely
   answer it.

4. If possible, I would involve a patient in a 1 2 3 4
   decision concerning him or her.

5. It is not my place, as a student, to make 1 2 3 4
   decisions.

This example is taken from an evaluation of students' affective learning in a department of nursing at the college level. It illustrates a different use of the rating scale. Students respond to the statements, not an observer.

Here are some guidelines for preparing rating scales.

- Write clear, unambiguous items which are as little open to interpretation as possible.

- Include only one behavior or characteristic in each item and base each item on an objective.

- Design a response scale which matches the nature of the evaluation being done—frequency of behaviors, quality of performance, or agreement with the statements.

- Include an equal number of positive and negative points on the scale. An unequal number influences the accuracy of the rating.

- Keep the number of items to a minimum. For use during an observation, there should be fewer than 15 items. When students are to respond to the statements, have fewer than 30.

- Arrange items in a logical sequence. Design a format that is not overcrowded or confusing.

Comments, Anecdotal Records, and Journals Comments, anecdotal records, and journals are used primarily in informal evaluation to provide feedback to students. Students or the instructor record comments on learning, how they feel about the situation in which they are working, or questions they have. We may keep anecdotal records in a group where participation or interaction among individuals is considered important. Simple notes about who speaks and perhaps something on the quality or content of their contribution suffice.

Journals can be used in a variety of ways. Students can first record what happened, then step back from the experience, view it in a fresh way, and question the value or importance of their reactions. In some situations, where the instructor is unable to participate or observe the learning experiences, students can keep a journal in which they describe what they did and what they learned. A social work student doing volunteer fieldwork might record his interactions with clients and describe how they are related to theoretical models.

Example 1:

In your journal, record at the end of each volunteer experience, your interaction with the client and how you felt or what you learned. Use the format illustrated below. Each Friday give your week's journal to your instructor for comments and feedback.

Record of Interaction	How I felt/What I learned
Client:	
Me:	
Client:	
Me:	

This example, taken from a first-year Skills Lab in a school of social work, illustrates a semi-structured journal. Learners are not expected to recall word for word their dialogue with a client, but it is expected that students learn to recall interactions as a part of their professional responsibility. In the second column, students are encouraged to record any cognitive learning, including what skill they were using, or affective learning, involving their personal reaction to the situation. Such journals are not usually graded, but used as an opportunity to provide detailed feedback.

Example 2:

Date	Name	Comment on Contribution

This example illustrates an anecdotal record form which could be used by an instructor interested in the frequency and the nature of individuals' contributions to group discussions. Such a record could form a component of the evaluation for grading purposes, if deemed relevant, or could be used to give feedback to individuals on their contributions.

Although comments, anecdotal records, and journals are usually informal evaluation techniques and are devised in a wide range of forms, some general guidelines for their use can be given.

- Plan which behaviors or responses should be recorded, based on the objectives.
- Design a format for the recording of comments and give directions for its use.
- Indicate whether comments to be recorded are to be objective (the "what" or "how" of the situation) or subjective (interpretations).
- Describe the context in which the information is collected or ask students to include this in their records.
- Ensure that the recording occurs either during or as soon as possible after the event.
- If the records contribute to grades, plan in advance specific criteria that will be used in the analysis of the results.

Arts-Based Evaluation Arts-based learning has become popular in adult education in recent years (for example, see Hoggan, Simpson and Stuckey, 2009). Although little has been written about incorporating arts-based evaluation into teaching and learning in adult education, it is a relatively small step to move from arts-based learning to arts-based evaluation. In a volume edited by Lawrence (2005), authors describe how music can be used to emphasize the cultural context of second language learners; poetry (found poems, read poems, and made poems) are a central part of a course on action research for teachers; and storytelling and photography are used in a "community for social justice project," to give a few examples. Arts-based activities can also demonstrate individuals' learning, especially when the educator is interested in affective learning, transformative learning, and self-directed learning.

In my teaching at the graduate and undergraduate levels and in my workshops, I offer the following kinds of options for either formal or informal evaluation of learning:

- Create a drawing, painting, or collage that represents your learning.
- Write a short story or poem that tells the reader about your learning in this course.
- Create a sculpture in any medium that is symbolic of your learning.
- Write a song, create a music CD of favorite pieces of music, perform or sing a musical piece that shows something about your learning.
- Prepare and perform a dance routine (videotaped or live) to show the stages of your learning.
- Work in a small group to create and perform a short play that represents your learning.

I also suggest that participants develop other creative and artistic ways to demonstrate their learning. Among their projects have been a creative web site, a quilt, a welding sculpture, an illustrated cookbook, and a design and blueprint for a garden.

Evaluating Learning in the Online Context Software platforms for web-based teaching and learning include tools to facilitate testing and grading online. These are usually in the form of quizzes and objectively-scored tests in different formats. For grading, there often is a system for keeping track of scores on quizzes and tests and converting them into a grade. In other words, the software supports traditional testing and grading of student learning. There are also mechanisms by which educators can grade or give points for learners' engagement in discussions (based on quality or quantity or both).

Not very much about evaluation of learning in online contexts is included in the literature. Some authors advocate the use of e-portfolios (for example, Abrami and Barrett, 2005) and claim that there needs to be an alternative to traditional testing models in the online environment. There are software applications that support the development of e-portfolios within courses. An e-portfolio has the same purpose as a regular learning portfolio—that is, it is a collection of evidence from a variety of sources that demonstrates the individual's learning. However, it is an electronic collection, and as such can include not only text, but also images, blogs, multimedia presentations and links to other sites. An e-portfolio can be updated over time and maintained throughout different courses or workshops. It encourages self-reflection at the same time as it provides evidence of learning.

Online learning also enables learners to easily collaborate on projects to demonstrate learning. King (2010) advocates dialogue and collaboration as the core concepts and she links this to assessment. She also suggests that different types of assessment may be appropriate online, but does not elaborate. One example of a collaborative project that students in my courses frequently do is a dialogue journal, where two or more students keep a journal in the form of letters to each other; another example is a group project where individuals set up a common worksite online so that each person can contribute, edit, and work on the project.

Essentially, all traditional forms of evaluation of learning can be transferred to the online environment, but in addition, educators can take advantage of the features of learning online to incorporate more collaborative learning projects and e-portfolios.

Summary

What makes evaluation of learning difficult and uncomfortable? I suspect unease occurs when educators are not sure that they are doing a good job. Learning takes place in a student's mind and body. We look at that student's work, listen to her talk, read what she writes, and make a judgment about the amount and quality of her learning. We often do not know what she knew before she started nor how much effort it cost her to get where she did during our teaching. Although we may design objectively scored instruments and try our hardest to be fair and equitable in our judgments, we are always interpreting and judging another person. I think this is hard for teachers who care about their students.

In this chapter, I present a systematic approach to evaluation that can enable us to be as fair and helpful as possible. And, the more we can involve students in the evaluation process, either through self-evaluation or participation in decision making regarding evaluation, the better we can alleviate our own evaluation anxieties.

We first need to consider our general approach to evaluation. Is it formal, leading to an official grade, or informal, leading to feedback or unofficial records? Should we use a norm-referenced model, comparing students to an external norm, or a criterion-referenced model, determining whether students meet a standard or criterion? Do we want to use an instructor evaluation or student self-evaluation process or some combination of the two? These may not be dichotomous decisions, but we should think through the approaches carefully.

Selection of specific evaluation techniques is based primarily on the nature of the learning. Some techniques are appropriate only for lower level cognitive learning. Complex, high level learning requires using open, subjectively rated formats, despite the time needed for marking. We also need to consider some student characteristics in our choice of evaluation techniques. While practical constraints may act as obstacles to using the ideal approach, we must try our best to match the evaluation to the learning.

The next thing to choose is a grading system if we must submit grades. Grades may be norm-referenced or criterion-referenced, though I hardly ever recommend the former. Contract grading does allow us to negotiate grades in advance with students, so that everyone understands the expectations. Self-evaluation gives the students varying degrees of control over the grading process. Using a matrix of objectives by evaluation techniques can be helpful to ensure that we are actually evaluating everything we expect students to learn.

The final and biggest job is to prepare the instruments, tests, or strategies to be used in evaluating student learning. I give examples of each of the commonly used techniques and guidelines for designing them. If we continually try to be clear, fair, considerate, and respectful of our students, while honestly evaluating what we expect them to learn, we will progress a long way toward good evaluation of learning.

Chapter 8
Evaluating Instruction

As instructors work with students, they often informally evaluate what is going on. While lecturing to a large group, a professor is aware of student unrest, lack of response, or a drop in attendance, and will modify his or her approach to regain the students' interest. A workshop leader who sees people are not participating in exercises or contributing to discussions quickly realizes that something needs to be changed. When students do not understand the concepts being presented in class, teachers try to explain in a different way, add examples, or switch to a different teaching method. They continually tune into the reactions and responses of a group, adapt, adjust, and revise what they do. Reflective practitioners not only review each class or session after it is over, but also reflect while teaching and intuitively respond to the ever-changing situation in the classroom.

As invaluable as informal and on-going evaluation of instruction is, we also need a more comprehensive and systematic evaluation of our practice for at least three reasons. First, there are increasing demands for accountability of educators in all contexts. Many colleges and universities now see themselves as accountable to business and industry for the quality of the training they provide. Universities are called upon to be accountable to their funding agencies whose resources diminish each year. Adult education programs in all contexts strive to attract students by ensuring the provision of meaningful and relevant learning experiences. Second, within educational institutions, the evaluation of teaching plays a critical role in hiring, renewal of contracts, and promotion. Although many university faculty are judged primarily on the basis of their research productivity, teaching evaluations now play a more important role in employing, continuing, and promoting personnel (for example, see Knapper, 1997). In colleges and adult education programs in general, teaching is now almost always systematically evaluated. Third, comprehensive evaluation provides educators with the information essential for their own professional growth and development.

Knowledge of teaching falls primarily into the communicative domain: it involves communicating with others within a social context. Evaluating teaching competence, therefore, is a subjective process, just as subjective rating is used to evaluate student learning in the higher levels of the cognitive domain or the affective domain. This makes teachers nervous. In the same way that some students complain about the validity or fairness of teacher ratings of essays, teachers worry about student ratings of teaching. However, the complexity of the teaching process means that it can only be evaluated subjectively—there is no alternative. Good subjective evaluations are trustworthy and credible (Patton, 2002). They depend on the expertise, professionalism, and credibility of the raters, as well as negotiation and agreement among individuals.

In this chapter, I provide a systematic approach to planning for the evaluation of instruction, which includes: a) clarifying the purpose of the evaluation; b) selecting the aspects of instruction to be evaluated; c) finding good sources of information; d) choosing techniques for collecting information; e) setting criteria; and, f) collecting and interpreting information. I strongly recommend that more than one source of information be used so that the perspective of one rater, whether an individual or a group, does not dominate the results. Subjectively rated evaluations benefit from a process called triangulation, in which information is collected from at least three sources and results are crosschecked. In the last part of the chapter, I recommend and discuss the use of teaching portfolios, in which educators collect evidence of the quality of their work for presentation to others.

Planning for Evaluating Instruction

When faced with the task of evaluating their instruction, many educators start with a student rating form. They may ask a colleague what form he uses and adapt that, or, if a committee is planning an evaluation procedure for a department or program, they may begin by generating items for a survey. This is akin to selecting a test format for students without knowing what learning is expected. It is helpful to systematically plan the evaluation of instruction.

Purpose of the Evaluation Evaluation of instruction has two primary purposes: to improve teaching and to contribute to administrative decisions on program and personnel. Although these purposes often overlap in practice, it should be clear from the outset how evaluation results will be used. Evaluation for improvement, to be meaningful, must yield information that is specific and detailed enough to tell the educator what needs to be changed. Evaluation for administrative decision making usually requires more general information, that is, overall assessments of quality. Most readers of this book, however, are concerned with planning their own instruction and will be interested in evaluation for improvement and development. Although this is the main focus in this section of the chapter, the same planning procedure can be used to design an evaluation for administrative decision making.

Aspects of Instruction to be Evaluated Evaluative information can be collected to confirm teaching strengths, clarify suspected weaknesses, or check out the effectiveness of a new strategy, activity, or reading. For convenience, I separate aspects of instruction into aspects of the course (or workshop, seminar, or other format) and aspects of teaching performance, though in practice this distinction need not be maintained.

Course Components. A good course design includes a list of objectives, a well-thought out sequence of instruction, a variety of teaching methods, appropriate materials, and effective techniques for evaluating students. Any of these course components can be evaluated, along with institutional and course resources and facilities. Each of the following components should be carefully considered for inclusion in an evaluation.

- Clarity and relevance of the objectives.
- Logic of the sequence of the topics.
- Effectiveness of the teaching methods.
- Inclusion of special methods, such as modules, online segments of instruction, or field trips.
- Quality of such materials as readings and books.
- Inclusion of media, either audio or visual.
- Use of outside resources, such as guest speakers, clinical facilities, or library services.
- Adequacy of internal resources, such as labs, computer facilities, or the physical environment.
- Provision of assignments and projects.
- Use of techniques for providing feedback.
- Quality of evaluation and testing procedures.
- Appropriateness of grading procedures.

Generally, the course components that are evaluated should be those that can be changed or revised. There is no point in finding out that everyone hates the room you are working in if no other room is available; in fact, it frustrates everyone to ask for feedback when nothing can be done about the situation. Neither is it wise to evaluate all aspects of a course at once. The evaluation becomes too long and complex, and it is too hard to make a large number of changes in any one situation.

Teaching Performance. The second aspect of instruction to be considered is the actual teaching performance—our behavior with students. Although teaching styles and roles vary considerably from one individual to another and from one instructional situation to another, there are several basic teaching skills that are important in any context. To some extent, researchers have identified the underlying components of effective teaching. The general consensus is that there are four major factors: a) presentation skill—the ability to convey information in a clear, interesting, relevant, and stimulating manner; b) rapport with learners—the ability to establish and maintain empathy with, concern for, and interaction with the group; c) structure — the ability to create and follow a definite outline or schedule that facilitates learning; and, d) the provision of feedback or the use of fair evaluation strategies. More specifically, we should consider each of the following components of teaching performance for inclusion in an evaluation.

- Establishing learner expectations.
- Organizing content logically.
- Pacing.
- Clarifying or developing an idea or topic (i.e., elaboration).
- Selecting the appropriate level of difficulty or challenge.
- Facilitating learner participation.
- Relating to learners' experiences (i.e. establishing a frame of reference).
- Asking questions.
- Responding to questions.
- Integrating ideas at the end of a session (i.e., closure).
- Using a variety of methods and materials.
- Showing creativity and innovation in teaching methods.
- Displaying flexibility and individualization.
- Managing time and activities.
- Establishing interpersonal relations.
- Creating a learning environment.
- Stimulating interest and enthusiasm.
- Identifying and clarifying values.
- Encouraging self-directed learning.
- Evaluating and providing feedback of learning.

It is important not to try to evaluate everything at once and to be sure that the time and resources exist to make improvements to the aspects that are evaluated.

Sources of Information   The third step in planning the evaluation of instruction comprises the selection of appropriate sources of information for the aspects of instruction under evaluation. Students should always be included as a source since they are most closely involved in and affected by the instruction, but they may lack the expertise to provide information on some aspects of a course or the teaching. I recommend that more than one source of information be used, preferably at least three, to provide an effective means of crosschecking the results. Since all evaluation of teaching is subjectively rated, each source provides a unique perspective.

- *Colleagues* can make judgments about course content, materials, resources, and organization.

- *Administrators* can affirm or question the relevance of instruction to the program.

- *Instructors* can reflect on the quality of their teaching and the amount of student learning achieved.

- *Learners* can offer ratings of the quality of teaching and their relationship with the educator, comment on the difficulty level, relevance of the content, and clarity of the objectives, and state how much they think they learned.

- *Previous students* can report on the relevance of the instruction to their professions, careers, or trades.

- *Individuals who dropped out or left the instruction* can offer opinions on the quality of teaching and relevance of the content.

- *Professional Associations* can indicate the relevance of the instruction to their professions.

- *Community agencies* can discuss the relevance of the instruction, current employment trends, and the type of training required.

- *Government agencies* can specify curriculum and professional requirements.

- *Other institutions* can comment on the content and organization of the course.

- *Support services* can offer information on library and computer facilities, drop-in centers, or counseling services.

Whether or not a source of information is appropriate depends on the context of the instruction, what we are evaluating, and why we are evaluating it. If we want to know whether a professional development workshop for nurses is working well, previous participants who have completed the workshop may provide valuable information, and the professional association will be able to judge the relevance of the content of the workshop. On the other hand, in a university-level course in the arts, students may give us the best information about the quality of teaching, and colleagues may be able to provide the best feedback on the materials and resources used in the course.

Techniques for Collecting Information

When we think of evaluating instruction, questionnaires most often come to mind. This tool does provide a quick and reliable way of getting information, but it also has limitations and should not be relied on exclusively. There are many techniques, and each yields a different type of information: much more detail can be obtained from an interview or discussion than from a rating scale; open-ended comments reveal unexpected reactions; videotapes provide a means of systematically observing teaching behavior. I describe the most commonly used techniques and give some information on the selection or development of each.

Interviews Interviews are face-to-face individual question and answer sessions. They may be preplanned and fairly structured or completely open-ended and flexible. They are most appropriate for obtaining information that cannot be easily quantified or for uncovering unexpected feelings and reactions. They generally provide detailed, in-depth information on a small number of topics and address the "why" rather than the "what" questions. Interviews can be held with small subgroups of students from a larger class in order to save time, but these then may not be completely representative of student reactions. Interview data of any kind are time-consuming and difficult to analyze but yield rich results.

A variety of interview formats can be used. In a structured or a semi-structured format, the questions are planned in advance, including follow-up questions or probes. The areas to be covered in the interview are based on the aspects of instruction being evaluated. In an open or unstructured interview, one general question or comment starts the discussion and the participant's responses lead the process from there. In an open interview, it is more difficult to ensure that each of the aspects of instruction to be evaluated is included. When interviews are carried out with small groups rather than with individuals, more structure is helpful. In small groups, people's responses will be stimulated by the general discussion, but some individual voices may be overlooked if we are not careful to include everyone. Consider the following when conducting evaluative interviews.

- It may be preferable for someone outside the course to conduct the interviews, especially if there is reason to believe that students would not feel completely comfortable being interviewed by the instructor or another student.

- Interviews should be as brief as possible while still eliciting the information needed.

- It is helpful to audiotape interviews. If this is not possible, a system for taking detailed notes should be devised.

- In a semi-structured or structured format, the questions should be specific and direct.

- Questions should be clear and jargon-free.

- The interviewer must be flexible. The most useful information is sometimes obtained when people have an opportunity to express themselves freely at some point during the interview.

- The interviewer should not express her or his own opinions.

- If interviews are conducted in small groups, interaction among the group members should be encouraged.

Observations Having someone watch the instruction in progress provides a valuable perspective. Observations may be fairly formal, wherein specific behaviors are observed and recorded or perhaps even rated. Checklists or rating scales (see Chapter Seven) can be used. Observations may also be rather informal—a colleague may sit in on a class or two and discuss what he or she noticed after the observation. Generally, though, observations are most useful for obtaining detailed information on specific teaching behaviors and skills. They are time-consuming but yield meaningful and sometimes surprising information. Bear the following in mind when using observation as an evaluation tool.

- It is best to decide in advance of the observation what the observer is looking for, even when it is an informal process. Selecting two or three aspects of instruction makes the observer's task easier.

- It is usually better if the observer knows in advance the teacher's intent for the session.

- If an instructional developer is available, he or she usually has experience observing classes and can make good, informed judgments.

- If the observer knows the content, she will be better suited to comment on the organization of the session, relationships among topics, and other content-related issues. If she is not familiar with the subject, she is better able to judge the skill of the teaching techniques, as she will not be attending primarily to the material itself.

- A checklist or rating scale may be helpful. However, I have found that general note-taking is easier and just as likely to yield useful results.

- Students should be informed about the observer's role in the class.

- Discussion about the observation should take place as soon as possible after the session while it remains fresh in everyone's mind.

- On some occasions, it can be useful for the observer to hold a discussion with students, either about the observation or to gather more information from a different perspective.

Comments Student comments provide extremely valuable information. Midway through a course, and sometimes even weekly, I ask students to respond in writing to four or five open-ended questions. I respond to the same questions myself, summarize the results, and give the summaries back to students for discussion.

Students appreciate being asked and especially enjoy the opportunity to see what everyone else said and discuss what changes should be made.

Another strategy is what I called the Quick Check Feedback (Cranton, 2003). I distribute blank index cards during the last few minutes of a class and ask students to respond anonymously to two questions, one on the front of the card and one on the back. The questions are general: "What are you enjoying in this course?" and "What would you like to see changed in future sessions?"

Following are some things to consider when using comments.

- Eliciting comments frequently, perhaps in every class, may prevent problems from going unnoticed, but becomes tedious for students.

- It is best if students submit their comments anonymously; however, in small classes where we soon recognize everyone's handwriting, this may be impossible.

- The questions asked or the areas in which comments are invited should be specific enough to yield information upon which to act.

- There is usually no need to conduct a formal analysis of comments. Summarizing the results and noting the frequency of similar responses is adequate.

- It is essential that student comments are taken seriously and that the instructor responds through discussion and/or making changes based on what has been written.

- We have a tendency to place more weight on negative comments. It is important not to overreact to one negative voice, although it should be taken seriously.

Questionnaires Student rating forms or questionnaires are the most commonly used technique for evaluating instruction. They usually include statements which students are asked to rate on a scale. Often students are also encouraged to respond to open-ended questions. In large groups, questionnaires are quick, practical, and generally reliable. Questionnaires often carry more weight than comments or other qualitative assessments in administrative decision making, simply because our culture values quantification.

However, questionnaires do not allow the respondent as much freedom in commenting as do interviews or unstructured comments, and therefore do not evoke unexpected reactions.

Student rating forms are often standardized for an institution, program, or department and administered by someone other than the educator. However, it is worth considering creating or finding a form that is specific to a course or context to use in addition to the form designed for administrative decision-making. Rating forms are available on the Internet or by sending an inquiry to a list service, such as the Professional and Organizational Development or the Society for Teaching and Learning in Higher Education. Published instruments or items have usually been tested for reliability and validity, but they may not match an individual educator's style or context.

Following are some guidelines for developing and using student questionnaires.

- Statements on a questionnaire should be clear and unambiguous.
- There should not be more than 30 statements on a student rating form.
- Only one behavior or characteristic should be addressed by each item.
- A response scale should contain between three and seven points, and each should be clearly labeled.
- There should be an equal number of positive and negative points on a response scale.
- The response scale must match the statements, both grammatically and in regard to meaning. Common response scales include: strongly agree, agree, disagree, strongly disagree; or, excellent, good, poor, unacceptable; or, almost always, often, sometimes, almost never.
- Questionnaires are less useful in very small classes.
- Some course characteristics, such as the size of the class and whether it is required or elective, have been shown to influence ratings.

- Student ratings can be influenced by special events in a course, such as a field trip or examination.
- Making comparisons between teachers in different courses based on student ratings is inadvisable.
- We have a tendency to over-interpret small differences among items on student questionnaires. The quantification of the results produces a false sense of precision.
- If questionnaire results are to be used for administrative decision making, it is a good idea to use a standardized procedure to administer the questionnaire. The teacher should not be in the room; a student or a third party should collect the questionnaires.

Student Learning Measures of participants' learning may be used as one indication of instructional effectiveness. We can consider formal test results or student papers, journals, or demonstrations as evidence of the quality of teaching. It is important to remember, however, that many things influence student learning so that it should never be the sole criterion for evaluating instruction. Guidelines for evaluating student learning are contained in Chapter Seven.

Content and Task Analysis One way of evaluating course materials, such as objectives, syllabi, or notes, is to conduct a content or task analysis. These procedures allow us to check the organization and comprehensiveness of the materials. Asking a colleague or other subject expert to analyze a course syllabus can provide valuable insights, but it is a fairly onerous task to ask of others. Guidelines for conducting an analysis are available in Chapter Four.

Videotapes and Audiotape Recordings Video or audiotaping a session provides a lasting record of observations of instruction. We can review our own teaching, looking at specific behaviors or how certain methods are working. Reviewing a video or audiotape with a colleague or instructional development specialist can prove insightful. Sometimes other people see things that we cannot see ourselves. The presence of the video equipment or tape recorder may be disconcerting at first, but we and our students soon get used to it and carry on as usual. The points to consider listed for observations of instruction also apply for the use of recordings, but there are a few additional thoughts to keep in mind.

- Although it is natural to want to be at our best on a tape, we should not try to put on a show for the camera or tape recorder. This defeats the purpose of using the tapes in evaluations, especially if our purpose is to improve instruction.

- It is worthwhile to engage the help of an experienced person to do any videotaping.

- The recording should include student reactions, comments, and discussions.

- The video should be viewed or the tape listened to more than once. With videotape, on our first viewing we may focus on appearance and mannerisms rather than the details of teaching.

- Sharing the tape with another person, followed by discussion, is extremely helpful.

- In some circumstances, sharing the tape, or portions of it, with students as a basis for discussion is useful.

Setting Criteria for the Evaluation

Before collecting information, it is important to consider the criteria we will use to determine whether or not our instruction is working. This is not easy, but it certainly helps to make systematic decisions if we have pre-defined what is good and not so good. Many factors affect the teaching and learning process. It is possible, however, to set standards, or a range of standards, keeping in mind that evaluation of teaching can never be completely precise. Revisions can be made as we proceed.

When the purpose of an evaluation is the improvement of instruction, the consequences of a wrong decision are not serious. It is preferable to set high standards; at worst, this will lead to improvements that are not necessary. A general procedure is outlined below.

- Rank the aspects of instruction selected for evaluation, accompanied by the items or questions developed to evaluate those aspects, according to their importance. For example, in professional training, field experience may be the most important component of the instruction; in a small discussion session, skill as a discussion leader may have first priority.

- Considering the time and resources available, decide where changes are possible and how much we are willing to change. Some revisions will be more time-consuming than others. It is important to be practical in deciding how much can be done.

- For each aspect and source of information, we should try to predict the results based on our own perception of how things are going. This can be done in a fairly general way by considering whether we expect the responses to be positive, neutral, mixed, or negative.

- The actual criteria can be set in one or more of several ways:

  - We can specify percentages or frequencies of responses below which that aspect of instruction will be a candidate for change. For example, we might decide that if more than 30% of the students are dissatisfied with the sequence of topics, we will review and revise the sequence. Criteria should be set separately for each aspect of the instruction being evaluated, and all relevant sources of information should be considered.

  - If setting specific criteria seems too arbitrary, a range can be used. For example, the criterion for the evaluation of the workload in a college-level course might be that if between 30% and 50% of the questionnaire responses are negative, students will be interviewed to obtain further information.

  - We can specify the number of areas in which improvements will be made, regardless of the absolute level of the responses. For example, we might decide that the three aspects of instruction receiving the lowest evaluation results will be revised.

  - Discrepancies between expected or predicted ratings and obtained ratings can be used as criteria for change, or as an indication that further evaluation is required.

One of the most common fates of evaluation results is that they are not used. Planning the criteria in advance provides a stronger incentive to do something with the results we obtain.

Collecting and Interpreting Information

When the evaluation has been carefully planned, data collection and interpretation are usually straightforward. However, results can be influenced to some extent by the directions given during the administration of the questionnaire, the timing of the data collection, the anonymity of responses, and the environment in which the information is collected. Some general guidelines follow.

- Questionnaires and comments should be anonymous. If we want to follow up on responses, code names or numbers can be used.

- Provide clear and accurate directions for all respondents — students, colleagues, professional groups, or administrators. The purpose of the evaluation should be made clear, and people should be assured that their responses are completely confidential.

- If practical, someone from outside of the course or workshop should conduct interviews, discussions, and observations.

- Ensure that people have adequate time to fill out forms or make comments. For example, a questionnaire should not be administered as people are preparing to leave the room. Asking individuals to take a questionnaire home and mail it in or bring it back to the next class is an option, but usually not all of the forms are returned, leaving us with an unrepresentative sample of responses. Evaluation is an important part of instruction; it deserves time.

- Evaluation information should not be collected immediately before or after any unusual event, such as taking a test, viewing a film, hearing a guest speaker, or just prior to or after a holiday.

- Information should be collected only after students have had sufficient time to become familiar with content and instructor, but while there is still time to make changes.

- Information should be collected in a relaxed and comfortable setting. It is not, for example, a good idea to have students come to a special office, one by one, for an interview, unless this is a routine part of the course.

- Whenever possible, conduct cross-checking of evaluation information with another source. A colleague may find a course up-to-date and clear, but students who have less background in the subject may find it incomprehensible.

How we analyze the evaluation information obviously depends on the techniques we are using. Usually, summaries of responses are all that is needed—how many people answered each question in each way, or averages and some indication of the dispersion of the scores for student ratings. Some suggestions for analyzing information of different types follow below.

- Interview results can be summarized into categories or themes. When the interviews are structured or semi-structured, the categories can be determined in advance from the questions asked and modified as necessary. When the interviews are unstructured, categories can be created after reading through or listening to the responses. The summary of results then consists of the frequency of responses in each category, possibly accompanied by a file of sample answers.

- To conduct observations, checklists or rating scales of the behaviors or characteristics being evaluated may be used. To analyze the results, determine the frequencies of checks or ratings for each item. Less structured observations may be summarized in a written memo or report or perhaps conveyed through discussion with the observer.

- Analyzing comments or reviews is a process similar to that used with interview results. Responses are categorized and then summarized by determining how many statements fall into each category.

- Questionnaire results are usually presented using frequencies of responses for each point on the scale. Item means or averages are also commonly used, but they should not be used alone. For example, if everyone gives a rating of 4 on a question, the average will be 4, but this means something quite different if people gave ratings of 5 and 1, still leading to an average of 4. It is also important not to interpret small differences in average ratings. An average rating of 3.2 is usually not meaningfully different from an average rating of 3.4.

- Analyzing and interpreting student learning is dependent on how that learning has been assessed. We may use average test results, letter grades, anecdotal records, or samples of students' essays and projects.

- If content or task analyses have formed a part of our evaluation, normally nothing more needs to be done with these results. When the content analysis has been done by colleagues, look for discrepancies between their perspectives and our own. Or, we might want to check to see whether our evaluations of student learning validate the analysis.

- We can analyze videotapes and tape recordings of teaching in the same way as live observations. Since these provide a permanent record, it is possible to do a very thorough job by reviewing the tape several times, taking notes, and checking off the frequency of various behaviors.

- Interpreting our evaluation results should be done primarily on the basis of the criteria we developed. Sometimes, it becomes apparent that the predetermined criteria are not realistic. We then need to set aside the evaluation results and rethink the criteria. I believe it is also very valuable to call upon our intuition, feelings, and recollections of details in interpreting evaluation results. Sometimes a hunch or feeling can shed light on the numbers.

Teaching Portfolios

Collecting and presenting evidence of the quality of teaching from many different sources can soon become confusing. Teaching dossiers or portfolios are now widely advocated as a way of organizing evaluation results. Teaching portfolios often are included as part of a promotion or tenure application. They also provide a good way to document teaching for personal use. The idea of a teaching portfolio is not new. It was originally developed in the 1980s in response to a request from the Canadian Association of University Teachers for a list of the kinds of information a faculty member could use as evidence of good teaching. In recent years, teaching portfolios have become a standard way of presenting evidence of teaching effectiveness (for example, see Seldin, 2004).

There are at least three types of evidence that are commonly collected: products of good teaching such as student essays and learning projects; educator-developed materials, including a philosophy of teaching, course syllabi, websites, and teaching innovations of any kind; assessments from others, such as student ratings, colleague observations, and unsolicited letters and cards from students.

The portfolio should include a variety of types of evidence. Below are some examples.

- Documentation of what we have done, such as a list of courses taught, online courses, selected course outlines, samples of innovative activities or exercises, and examples of evaluation of learning.

- Evaluation information collected from a variety of sources, as described in the earlier part of this chapter.

- An overview of our professional development, including a statement of a philosophy of practice and how it has changed over time, a description of involvement in professional development sessions, comments from earlier evaluations and how they were addressed.

- Samples of publications or conference presentations related to teaching, and descriptions of any research on teaching conducted in the classroom.

Some guidelines on how to prepare a portfolio may also be useful.

- Collect information for a portfolio on an on-going basis. A simple system of file folders or a computer file to store course outlines, letters from students, and student-rating results is invaluable.

- Select information carefully. For example, not every course outline needs to be included, but the ones used should be representative of the teaching.

- Summarize student ratings in tables.

- Include verbatim examples of student responses to open-ended questions. A variety is best; interesting or unusual comments make the portfolio pleasurable to read.

- Unsolicited letters from students or memos from colleagues describing an observation of a class can be included verbatim, with the permission of the author of the material.

- A statement of philosophy of teaching should be short, less than one page, and express the essence of what teaching means.
- The overall dossier should not be an overwhelming size. It should be presented in a binder or portfolio, with a table of contents and tabs or markers to assist the reader in finding specific sections.
- E-portfolios are gaining in popularity and can be substituted for a paper copy. The guidelines as to the content and organization remain the same.

A good portfolio is interesting to read and presents our work in the best possible light, but without ignoring weaknesses. Areas in which we have improved should be pointed out, along with plans for further developmental work.

Summary

In business and industry, performance appraisals are routine and regarded as a natural part of the working world. In education, however, we have fought for a long time against the evaluation of instruction, arguing that the teaching process is too complex to be assessed or that students cannot judge the quality of instruction until long after their course or program is completed, if at all. I believe that our opposition is largely due to our awareness that teaching knowledge is primarily communicative in nature and therefore cannot be evaluated using the objective or scientific methods appropriately applied to other domains of performance. While we may feel uneasy asserting that evaluation of teaching is, or even must be, subjective, we are equally uneasy trying to quantify it. As educators become more familiar with qualitative paradigms as a way of understanding the teaching and learning process in research, we also may become more accepting of qualitative approaches to evaluating instruction. The recent popularity of the teaching portfolio demonstrates this change in thinking.

In this chapter, I emphasize the importance of using a systematic approach to evaluating instruction, gathering information from several sources, using a variety of techniques, and documenting evidence of quality in a portfolio.

The purpose of the evaluation, whether for professional development, administrative decision making, or some combination of the two, determines what kind of questions we need to ask, especially their degree of specificity. The purpose needs to be clarified at the outset.

Just as we evaluate student learning according to objectives, we need to select carefully the aspects of instruction we want to evaluate, including such components as the course methods and materials or specific teaching skills on which we want feedback. Depending on what we are evaluating, we can then choose the best sources of information for what we need. Colleagues, for example, can assess the content, materials, and resources in a course, while students can tell us if they are motivated, interested, and able to learn in the teaching environment.

Although we tend to equate the widely used student questionnaires with evaluating instruction, many other techniques are available to collect in-depth information and provide us with a more complete picture of the quality of our work. Interviews, comments, observations, and videotapes of teaching each provide a different perspective.

In order to make the most of evaluation information, it is very helpful to consider criteria for interpreting the results in advance of gathering them.

The collection, analysis, and interpretation of evaluation information follow naturally from a good plan. Qualitative information, especially, requires time and consideration to make the most of what it has to tell us about our teaching.

I strongly recommend that educators design a teaching portfolio early in their careers and maintain it regularly. A teaching portfolio is a collection of materials related to our teaching, evaluation information, and developmental activities and plans. It not only allows us to communicate with others about what we do, but also creates a representative and in-depth picture of our teaching career for our own use.

References

Abrami, P.C., and Barrett, H. (2005). Directions for research and development on electronic portfolios. *Canadian Journal of Learning and Technology* 31 (3).

Allen, I.E., and Seaman, J. (2008). *Staying the course: Online education in the United States, 2008.* Needham, MA: Sloan Consortium.

Archer, W., and Garrison, D.R. (2010). Distance education in the age of the internet. In C. E. Kasworm, A. D. Rose, and J. M. Ross-Gordon, eds., *Handbook of adult and continuing education.* Thousand Oaks, CA: Sage.

Ausubel, D. P. (1968). *Educational psychology: A cognitive view.* New York: Holt, Rinehart, and Winston.

Ausubel, D. P. and Fitzgerald, D. (1961). The role of discriminability in meaningful verbal learning and retention. *Journal of Educational Psychology,* 52, 266-274.

Bee, H. L. (1995). *The journey of adulthood,* 3rd ed. New York: Macmillan.

Belenky, M. F., Clinchy, B.M., Goldberger, N.R., and Tarule, J.M. (1986). *A tradition that has no name.* New York: Basic Books.

Belenky, M.F., and Stanton, A. (2000). Inequality, development, and connected knowing. In Mezirow, J., and Associates, eds., *Learning as transformation: Perspectives on a theory in progress*. San Francisco: Jossey-Bass.

Bloom, B. (1956). *Taxonomy of educational objectives, Handbook I: Cognitive domain*. New York: McKay.

Boje, D.M (2008). *Storytelling organizations*. Thousand Oaks, CA: Sage.

Boucouvalas, M., and Lipson-Lawrence, R. (2010). Adult learning. In C. E. Kasworm, A. D. Rose, and J. M. Ross-Gordon, eds., *Handbook of adult and continuing education* (pp. 35-48). Thousand Oaks, CA: Sage.

Brookfield, S. D. (1986). *Understanding and facilitating adult learning*. San Francisco: Jossey-Bass.

——— (2005). *The power of critical theory*. San Francisco: Jossey-Bass.

——— (2006). *The skillful teacher: On technique, trust, and responsiveness in the classroom,* 2nd ed. San Francisco: Jossey-Bass.

——— (2010). Theoretical frameworks for understanding the field. In C. E. Kasworm, A. D. Rose, and J. M. Ross-Gordon, eds., *Handbook of adult and continuing education*. Thousand Oaks, CA: Sage.

Brookfield, S.D., and Preskill, S. (1999). *Discussion as a way of teaching*. San Francisco: Jossey-Bass.

Caffarella, R. S. (2002). *Planning programs for adult learners: A practical guide for educators, trainers, and staff developers,* 2nd ed. San Francisco: Jossey-Bass.

Caffarella, R.S., and Olson, S. (1993). Psychosocial development of women. *Adult Education Quarterly* 43, 125-151.

Candy, P. C. (1991). *Self-direction for lifelong learning: A comprehensive guide to theory and practice*. San Francisco: Jossey-Bass.

Cervero, R. M. and Wilson, A. L. (2006). *Working the planning table: Negotiating democratically for adult, continuing, and workplace education.* San Francisco: Jossey-Bass.

Clark, M. C., and Rossiter, M. (2008). Narrative learning in adulthood. In S. Merriam, ed., *Third update on adult learning theory.* New Directions for Adult and Continuing Education, no. 119. San Francisco: Jossey-Bass.

Cohen, L. R. (1999). Strategies for sequencing instruction. Personal communication.

Collins, M. (1998). Critical returns: From andragogy to lifelong education. In Scott, S. M., Spencer, B., and Thomas, A. M., eds., *Learning for life: Canadian readings in adult education.* Toronto: Thompson Educational Publishing.

Crandall, B., Klein, G., and Hoffman, R. (2006). *Working minds: A practitioner's guide to cognitive task analysis.* Cambridge: MIT Press.

Cranton, P. (1996). Types of group learning. In S. Imel, ed., *Learning in groups: Exploring fundamental principles, new uses, and emerging opportunities.* New Directions in Adult and Continuing Education, no. 71. San Francisco: Jossey-Bass.

———— (2001). *Becoming an authentic teacher in higher education.* Malabar, FL: Krieger.

———— (2003). *Finding our way: A guide for adult educators.* Toronto: Wall & Emerson.

———— (2006). *Understanding and promoting transformative learning: A guide for educators of adults,* 2nd ed. San Francisco: Jossey-Bass.

———— (2010). Transformative learning in an online environment. *International Journal of Adult Vocational Education and Technology,* 1(2), 1-10.

Cranton, P., and Knoop, R. (1995). Assessing psychological type: The PET Type Check. *General, Social, and Genetic Psychological Monographs*, 121(2), 247-274.

Cronbach, L.J. (1957). The two disciplines of scientific psychology. *American Psychologist*, 12, 671–684.

Degitz, L. (1999). Strategies for sequencing learning. Personal communication.

Dewey, J. (1916). *Education and democracy.* New York: Macmillan.

———— (1938). *Experience and Education.* London: Collier Macmillan

Dirkx, J. M., ed. (2008). *Adult learning and the emotional self.* New Directions for Adult and Continuing Education, no. 120. San Francisco: Jossey-Bass.

English, L. M., and Tisdell, E.J. (2010). Spirituality and adult education. In C. E. Kasworm, A. D. Rose, and J. M. Ross-Gordon, eds., *Handbook of adult and continuing education.* Thousand Oaks, CA: Sage.

Erickson, E. H. (1959). Identity and the life cycle. *Psychological Issues,* 1 (Monograph no. 1).

Fenwick, T. J. (2003). *Learning through experience: Troubling orthodoxies and intersecting questions.* Malabar, FL: Krieger.

Freiler, T. J. (2008), Learning through the body. In S. B. Merriam, ed., *Third update on adult learning theory.* New Directions for Adult and Continuing Education, no. 119. San Francisco: Jossey-Bass.

Freire, P. (1973). *Education for critical consciousness.* New York: Continuum Publishing.

———— (1994). *Pedagogy of hope.* New York: Continuum Publishing.

Gagné, R.M. (1975). *Essentials of learning for instruction.* Hinsdale, Illinois: Dryden Press.

———— (1977). *The conditions of learning*, 3rd ed. New York: Holt, Rinehart and Winston.

Galbraith, M. W. and Jones, M. S. (2010). Assessment and evaluation. In C. E. Kasworm, A. D. Rose, and J. M. Ross-Gordon, eds., *Handbook of adult and continuing education.* Thousand Oaks, CA: Sage.

Gardner, H. (1993). *Frames of mind: The theory of multiple intelligences,* 10th anniversary edition. New York: Basic Books.

Gardner, H., Kornhaber, M.L., and Wake, W.K. (1996). *Intelligence: Multiple perspectives.* New York: Harcourt Brace.

Gilligan, C. (1986). *In a different voice.* Cambridge: Harvard University Press.

Goleman, D. (1998). *Working with emotional intelligence.* New York: Bantam Books.

Grow, G. (1991). Teaching learners to be self-directed: A stage approach. *Adult Education Quarterly, 41,* 124-149.

Habermas, J. (1971). *Knowledge and human interests.* Boston: Beacon Press.

Hansman, C. A. and Mott, V. W. (2010). Adult learners. In C. E. Kasworm, A. D. Rose, and J. M. Ross-Gordon, eds., *Handbook of adult and continuing education.* Thousand Oaks, CA: Sage.

Hart, M. (2005). Class and gender. In T. Nesbit, ed., *Class concerns: Adult education and social class.* San Francisco: Jossey-Bass.

Hauenstein, A.D. (1998). *Conceptual framework for educational objectives: A holistic approach to traditional taxonomies.* Lanham, MD: University Press of America

Hoggan, C., Simpson, S., and Stuckey, H., eds. (2009). *Creative expression in transformative learning: Tools and techniques for educators of adults.* Malabar, FL: Krieger.

Jung, C. ([1921] 1971). *Psychological types.* Princeton: NJ: Princeton University Press.

Kasworm, C. E., Rose, A. D., and Ross-Gordon, J. M., eds. (2010). *Handbook of adult and continuing education.* Thousand Oaks, CA: Sage.

Kegan, R. (2000). What "form" transforms? A constructive-developmental approach to transformative learning. In J. Mezirow and Associates, eds., *Learning as transformation: Critical perspective on a theory in progress.* San Francisco, CA: Jossey-Bass.

Kegan, R., and Lahey, L. L. (2009). *Immunity to change: How to overcome it and unlock potential in yourself and your organization.* Boston: Harvard Business Press.

King, K. P. (2010). Where do I begin? Designing online learning courses that work. *International Journal of Adult Vocational Education and Technology,* 1, 14-30.

King, P. M., and Kitchener, K.S. (1994). *Developing reflective judgment.* San Francisco: Jossey-Bass.

Knapper, C. (1997). Rewards for teaching. In Cranton, P., ed., *Universal challenges in faculty work: Fresh perspectives from around the world.* New Directions for Teaching and Learning, no. 72. San Francisco: Jossey-Bass.

Knowles, M.S. (1978). *The adult learner: A neglected species,* 2nd ed. Houston: Gulf.

———— (1980). *The modern practice of adult education.* New York: Association Press.

———— (1984). *Andragogy in action: Applying modern principles of adult learning.* San Francisco: Jossey-Bass.

Kolb, D. (1984). *Experiential learning.* Englewood Cliffs, NJ: Prentice-Hall.

Krathwohl, D. (1998). *Appendix A: Summary of the changes from the original framework.* Pre-publication manuscript.

Krathwohl, D.R., Bloom, B.S., and Masia, B.B. (1964). *Taxonomy of educational objectives, Handbook II: Affective domain.* New York: McKay.

Lawrence, R. L., ed. (2005). *Artistic ways of knowing: Expanded opportunities for teaching and learning.* New Directions for Adult and Continuing Education, no. 107. San Francisco: Jossey-Bass.

Lin, L. (2006). Cultural dimensions of authenticity in teaching. In P. Cranton, ed., *Authenticity in teaching.* New Directions for Adult and Continuing Education, no. 111. San Francisco: Jossey-Bass.

Lindeman, E. (1926). *The meaning of adult education.* Montreal: Harvester House.

MacKeracher, D. (2004). *Making sense of adult learning,* 2nd ed. Toronto: University of Toronto Press.

Mayer, R. (2003) *Learning and instruction.* Upper Saddle River, NJ: Pearson Education, Inc.

McEnrue, M. P. and Groves, K. (2006). Choosing among tests of emotional intelligence: What is the evidence? *Human Resource Development Quarterly,* 17, 9-42.

Merriam, S. B., and Brockett, R. G. (2007). *The profession and practice of adult education.* San Francisco: Jossey-Bass.

Merriam, S. B., Caffarella, R. S., and Baumgartner, L. M. (2007). *Learning in adulthood: A comprehensive guide,* 3rd ed. San Francisco: Jossey-Bass.

Mezirow, J. (1977). Perspective transformation. *Studies in Adult Education,* 9, 100–110.

———— (1981). A critical theory of adult learning and education. *Adult Education,* 32, no. 1.

————— (1991). *Transformative dimensions of adult learning.* San Francisco: Jossey-Bass.

Mezirow, J, and Taylor, E.W., eds. (2009). *Transformative learning in practice: Insights from community, workplace, and higher education.* San Francisco: Jossey-Bass.

Palmer, P. J. (2007). *The courage to teach: Exploring the inner landscape of a teacher's life,* 10th anniversary edition. San Francisco: Jossey-Bass.

Patton, M. Q. (2002). *Qualitative research and evaluation methods,* 3rd ed. Thousand Oaks, CA: Sage Publications.

Perry, W. G. (1999). *Forms of intellectual and ethical development in the college years: A scheme.* San Francisco: Jossey-Bass.

Pohl, M. (2000). *Learning to think, thinking to learn: Models and strategies to develop a classroom culture of chinking.* Cheltenham, Vic.: Hawker Brownlow.

Pratt, D. D. (1993). Andragogy after twenty-five years. In S. B. Merriam, ed., *An update on adult learning theory.* New Directions for Adult and Continuing Education, no. 57. San Francisco: Jossey-Bass.

Randall, W. L. (1996). Restorying a life: Adult education and transformative learning. In J.E. Birren et al., eds., *Aging and biography: Explorations in adult development.* New York: Springer.

Rogers, C.R. (1969). *Freedom to learn.* Columbus, Ohio: Merrill Publishing.

Rossiter, M., and Clark, M.C. (2007). *Narrative and the practice of adult education.* Malabar, FL: Krieger.

Seldin, P. (2004). *The teaching portfolio: A practical guide to improved performance and promotion/tenure decisions,* 3rd ed. Bolton, MA: Anker.

Shepherd, A. (2001). *Hierarchical task analysis.* New York: Taylor and Francis.

Simpson, E.J. (1966). The classification of educational objectives: Psycho-motor domain. University of Illinois Research Project no. OE 5, 85–104.

Smith, B. (1999). *The learning experiences of older adults as university students.* Unpublished doctoral dissertation. Toronto: University of Toronto.

Smith, R. O.(2008). Adult learning and the emotional self in virtual online contexts. In J. Dirkx, ed., *Adult learning and the emotional self.* New Directions for Adult and Continuing Education, no. 120. San Francisco: Jossey-Bass.

———— (2010). Facilitation and design of learning. In C. E. Kasworm, A. D. Rose, and J. M. Ross-Gordon, eds., *Handbook of adult and continuing education.* Thousand Oaks, CA: Sage.

Sork, T. J. (2010). Planning and delivering programs. In C. E. Kasworm, A. D. Rose, and J. M. Ross-Gordon, eds., *Handbook of adult and continuing education.* Thousand Oaks, CA: Sage.

Sork, T.J. and Newman, M. (2004). Program development in adult education and training. In G. Foley, ed., *Dimensions of adult learning: Adult education and training in a global era.* Crows Nest, NSW: Allen and Unwin.

Taylor, E. W. (2008). Transformative learning theory. In S. Merriam, ed., *Third update on adult learning theory.* New Directions for Adult and Continuing Education, no. 119. San Francisco: Jossey-Bass.

Taylor, E. W., and Cranton, P. (2012). *The Handbook of Transformative Learning: Theory, Research, and Practice.* San Francisco: Jossey-Bass.

Tisdell, E. J. (2007). In the new millennium: The role of spirituality and the cultural imagination in dealing with diversity and equity in the higher education classroom. *Teachers College Record,* 109, 531-560.

———— (2008). Spirituality and adult learning. In S. Merriam, ed., *Third update on adult learning theory.* New Directions for Adult and Continuing Education, no. 119. San Francisco: Jossey-Bass.

Tough, A. (1967). *Learning without a teacher.* Educational Research Series, no. 3. Toronto: Ontario Institute for Studies in Education.

———— (1979). *The adult's learning projects: A fresh approach to theory and practice in adult education.* Toronto: Ontario Institute for Studies in Education.

Vella, J. (2002). *Learning to listen, learning to teach.* San Francisco: Jossey-Bass.

Weathersby, R. (1981). Ego development. In A.W. Chickering, ed., *The modern American college.* San Francisco: Jossey-Bass.

Wilcox, S. (1995). Interview with George Geis. Personal communication.

Index